Sarah

MILLS & BOON®

Why shop at millsandboon.co.uk?

Each year, thousands of romance readers find their perfect read at millsandboon.co.uk. That's because we're passionate about bringing you the very best romantic fiction. Here are some of the advantages of shopping at www.millsandboon.co.uk:

* **Get new books first**—you'll be able to buy your favourite books one month before they hit the shops

* **Get exclusive discounts**—you'll also be able to buy our specially created monthly collections, with up to 50% off the RRP

* **Find your favourite authors**—latest news, interviews and new releases for all your favourite authors and series on our website, plus ideas for what to try next

* **Join in**—once you've bought your favourite books, don't forget to register with us to rate, review and join in the discussions

Visit **www.millsandboon.co.uk**
for all this and more today!

COLLINS GUIDE
TO
AQUARIUM FISHES
AND PLANTS

Text

Arne Schiotz

Illustrations

Preben Dahlstrom

Translated and Adapted by

Gwynne Vevers

Collins

London

William Collins Sons & Co. Ltd.
London · Glasgow · Sydney · Auckland · Toronto · Johannesburg

© in the English translation 1972 by William Collins Sons & Co. Ltd.,
London, and J. B. Lippincott Company
© in the Original Danish version 1969 by G. E. C. Gads Forlag, Copenhagen

ISBN 0 00 212004 6

Colour plates printed by F. E. Bording, Copenhagen
Filmset by Keyspools Ltd., Golborne, Lancashire, England
Made and printed in Great Britain by
William Collins Sons & Co. Ltd., Glasgow

FOREWORD

In this book our aim has been to give a basic, but popular account – fully illustrated in colour – of the main aquarium fishes and plants from fresh waters and the sea.

In selecting the species we have first and foremost paid attention to those which are regularly kept in the aquarium. There are also, however, many species which are only occasionally imported or which are no longer imported and of these we have tried to show some characteristic representatives.

The illustrations show the fishes – usually the most brightly coloured sex – in the colour pattern which they normally have under aquarium conditions, and only exceptionally the more brilliant juvenile coloration. A total of 406 fishes have been painted, of which 48 are females or juveniles. In addition some 53 plant species have been illustrated and the descriptions of these have been printed on a pale green background.

We thank K. Lindschouw Hansen who has very kindly placed a large number of the plants at our disposal.

The fact that it has been possible to paint the vast majority of the fishes from living specimens is due to the great help we have received from many private aquarists and dealers during the preparation of this book.

Some of the fishes were painted at the Copenhagen Aquarium Society's Exhibition in 1968, and we are grateful to J. V. Rasmussen for his help on this occasion. We would also like to thank J. J. Scheel for assistance with the section on cyprinodonts, and Mr Werner Schröder, Director of the Aquarium in West Berlin, and his staff for their hospitality during a pleasant and fruitful stay in Berlin, where certain rare species were painted.

Jens Meulengracht-Madsen has very kindly read the greater part of the text and checked most of the illustrations prior to their reproduction, and we are most grateful to him.

Preben Dahlstrom   *Arne Schiotz*

CONTENTS

Sarah Dickens

THE FISH

Appearance and structure 5
Colour and pattern 9
The relationship of fishes 12
Species and subspecies 14
Fish names 15
Distribution of fishes 16

FRESHWATER FISHES 17

BRACKISH-WATER
FISHES 140

MARINE FISHES 145

INVERTEBRATES 182

PLANTS 186
Algae 190

VISITORS 192

DISEASES 194

THE FRESHWATER
AQUARIUM 200
Technical aids 200
The water 203
The interior 204
Food and feeding 206
Breeding 208

THE MARINE AQUARIUM 210
The tank 210
The water 210
Food 212
Disease 213
Grouping the fishes 213
The interior 214

BIBLIOGRAPHY 215

INDEX 216

THE FISH

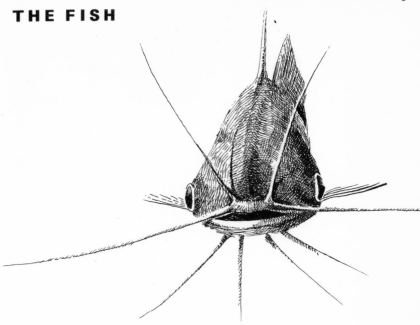

Appearance and Structure

The aquarist is primarily interested in the living fish and is less interested in the systematic zoologist's study of the preserved fish's external appearance (morphology) and its internal organs (anatomy). It is, however, useful for him to know certain morphological terms, since he often has to consult the literature in order to identify an aquarium fish. The illustration shown below explains some of the terms which may be of interest to the aquarist.

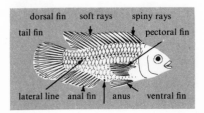

Fins

The forward movement and steering of a fish are effected by the muscular tail and by the fins, which are bony or cartilaginous outgrowths covered with thin skin. One can differentiate between the paired fins, the pectorals and ventrals which correspond to the fore and hind limbs of the higher vertebrates, and the unpaired fins – dorsal, caudal and anal. There may be more than one dorsal fin and in some fish families there is a small fleshy adipose fin behind the dorsal fin. For fast swimming most fish use the caudal fin and tail, whereas the pectorals and in some fishes the anal and dorsal are used for slower movements.

Some species, such as mudskippers and toadfishes, can use the paired fins almost as land animals use their limbs.

6

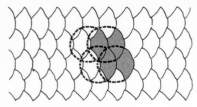

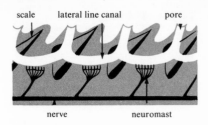

Vertical section through lateral line.

Scales

In most fishes the body is covered with scales over which there is a thin, mucus-covered layer of skin, which provides an effective barrier against the entry of disease-carrying organisms. When roughly handled a fish may lose a number of scales. This is not in itself so serious, because the scales regenerate, but the accompanying wound may allow the entry of serious infections.

Lateral line

In most fishes there is a more or less distinct line along the sides of the body. This is a characteristic organ known as the lateral line, a channel lying beneath the scales with side connections leading to the surface. This channel is richly supplied with nerve endings. By means of this organ

the fish can detect pressure waves and thus pick up the 'echo' produced when its own pressure waves are reflected by objects in the vicinity. This allows the fish to form a relatively good picture of the objects around it, even in dark or murky water. This is how blind fishes orientate themselves in an aquarium. Thus the lateral line functions much like the ear in higher vertebrates.

Anatomy

A certain knowledge of anatomy will be necessary if one is to dissect a fish. The drawing shown below is intended to help in such a dissection and to show the shape and relative positions of the main organs.

These organs are similar to the corresponding organs of higher animals and man, and in general they have the same shape and relative position.

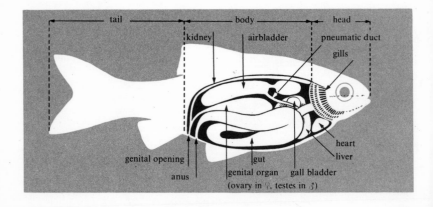

Swim bladder

The swim bladder, which is peculiar to the fishes, is an organ of buoyancy, permitting fishes to remain at various water depths. The amount of gas in this bladder can be changed by the action of a secretory and absorbing organ, so that the fish can always adjust its specific gravity to that of the water, independent of the depth.

The swim bladder has actually been evolved from the lungs possessed by the earliest fishes. In some fishes the air duct connects the swim bladder to the pharynx.

Gills

Fishes live in water and are able to utilize the oxygen dissolved in the water by means of the gills. These are thin-skinned, leaf-like structures with many small blood vessels, which allow the blood and the outside water to come into very close contact, so that an exchange of oxygen and carbon dioxide can take place. If the oxygen content of the water is higher than that of the blood, oxygen will diffuse into the blood. In most aquarium fishes the current of water flows over the gills because of rhythmic movements of the gill-covers and mouth. These movements will become more rapid as the oxygen content in the water falls. Rapid gill-cover movement is a clear warning that something may be wrong. Certain fast-swimming species do not actively move the gill-covers, but swim with the mouth open so that there is a constant flow of water over the gill filaments. These fishes must swim continuously, otherwise they would suffocate.

Some fishes feed on plankton caught by the gills; in these the gills are equipped with a series of gill-rakers which form a sieve. This method of feeding is only found in a few modern fishes, but it is thought that the original function of the gills was to sieve food from the water,

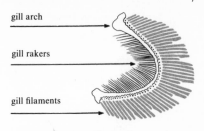

gill arch

gill rakers

gill filaments

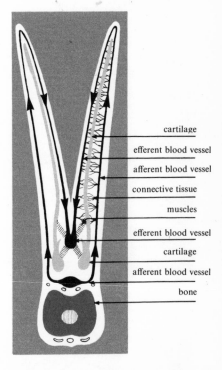

cartilage

efferent blood vessel

afferent blood vessel

connective tissue

muscles

efferent blood vessel

cartilage

afferent blood vessel

bone

Vertical section of a gill filament.

The blood supply to the gills enters as deoxygenated blood. The oxygenated blood leaves the gills and travels to the body.

and that it was only later that the gills became a respiratory organ. The first fishes breathed by means of lungs, but when the gills took over the respiratory function, the lung evolved into an organ of buoyancy, the swim bladder.

examples of body form

Body shape

The typical fish body is streamlined and torpedo-shaped, with the body's greatest cross section at a distance from the tip of the snout which is 36 per cent of the total length. This shape is found in those fishes which swim fast and for long periods with a minimal use of energy, such as herrings, mackerels and tunas in the open sea, species of *Brachydanio* and many species of *Rasbora* from rivers, and several others. But not all fishes need to move fast. Many other factors play a part in body shape. Fishes which live among vegetation, like the angelfish, or to a lesser extent many of the barbs, are often tall. Territorial fishes, which are seldom far from the nearest hiding hole, often have a compact, somewhat thickset body: e.g. cichlids and many coral-reef fishes.

Bottom-living fishes are often flat, either laterally compressed and lying on one side like the flat-fishes or eel-shaped if they live in a soft bottom or in crevices of rocky shores and reefs. Surface fishes often have a straight dorsal line and an upturned mouth, ready to snap up falling insects. The sea horse, moving slowly from one clump of seaweed to the next, resembles a tuft of seaweed, and pipe-fishes look like sticks.

Fishes living in running water are often shaped as though the current is pressing them against the bottom.

Puffers and boxfishes are slow-moving snail eaters, which are protected against their enemies by the possession of spines or by the ability to inflate themselves.

The shape of the body reflects a fish's way of life, and it often gives the aquarist a useful clue when he has to assess the requirements of a newly imported and unknown species.

Some examples of body shape are shown on the left.

COLOUR AND PATTERN

The beautiful colours and patterns of aquarium fishes play an important part in attracting the aquarist. But what is the function of colour and pattern? Scarcely to please the aquarist. Colour and pattern are by no means accidental. Certain principles are encountered again and again, not only in fishes but also in other animals. A couple of the most important principles can be mentioned here.

In nature there are two opposing principles. One is that an animal which blends as much as possible with its surroundings will be better able to avoid enemies or to approach its prey.

It may, on the other hand, be an advantage to show very bright colours and to have a body shape that is as conspicuous as possible, for these points attract the attention of the opposite sex and act as a threat to rivals. Which of these two principles gets the upper hand depends upon the fish's living conditions.

In open water, where there is nowhere to hide, a fish should be as inconspicuously coloured as possible, and so most species from there are coloured to blend with water and sky.

Fishes from flat, sandy bottoms, which may also have difficulty in finding a hiding-place, are normally sand-coloured.

On the other hand, if a fish lives on a coral reef or among dense vegetation, where it is never far to the nearest hiding-place, it can afford to have bright colours. But even for these fishes it may, in times of crisis, be an advantage to be able to become inconspicuous, and so the most brilliant coloration is usually combined with features which make the fish more difficult to distinguish.

Countershading

Since light always strikes the water from above, a fish's back tends to appear palest, with a gradual transition to the darker belly. Without some protection, an enemy would get a clear impression of the fish's rounded shape, even if the fish were in other respects coloured like its surroundings. To counteract this, fishes are dark above and pale on the belly. This, however, is seen only when the fish is uniformly illuminated; if lit from above it appears to be uniform in colour and thus appears flat. Enemies then have more difficulty in recognizing it as a rounded object, a fish.

This so-called countershading is natur-

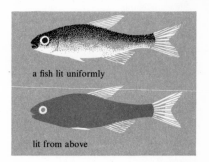

a fish lit uniformly

lit from above

ally seen most clearly in unicoloured fish, but it is found even in the most brightly coloured coral-reef fishes and also in numerous other animals. There are only a few fishes which apparently do not follow this rule. The upside-down catfish *Synodontis nigriventris* (p. 64) is palest on the back and darkest on the belly. But this apparent inconsistency is explained when one sees the fish in an aquarium, for it normally swims belly up.

Disruptive pattern

The striking dark patterns seen on many fishes appear to make them conspicuous, but only apparently so.

Patterns of this kind are called disruptive, and they correspond to the wartime camouflage of ships, tanks, etc. The outline by which one recognizes the animal concerned, which is visible even when the animal is protectively coloured, breaks up and therefore disappears. This tendency is further reinforced because the dark parts of the pattern appear to lie in another plane, farther back, than the paler parts. Even fishes that are all black and white, such as *Dascyllus trimaculatus* (p. 160) and *Plotosus lineatus* (p. 176) are almost impossible to recognize as fish when they are seen in nature, particularly when such strongly disruptive patterns are accompanied by close shoaling behaviour and sudden, swerving movements.

In such disruptive patterns it is very noticeable that the conspicuous markings usually run aross the contours of the animal, seldom along them.

Concealing the eyes

All animals react very strongly to a circular, dark spot, which is recognized as an eye, possibly because an eye which stares at one often denotes danger, and is perceived quite instinctively. Therefore

even the best countershading or disruptive pattern will be ineffective if a black, staring eye is continually visible. Many well-camouflaged land animals, such as fawns and the young of certain birds overcome this problem by closing their eyes when danger threatens; but fishes have no eyelids. In fishes the problem is frequently solved by having a dark streak running through the eye, so that the dark pupil forms part of the streak; this method is very commonly used. If you turn the pages of this book, especially to the section on coral-reef fishes, you will see that whenever a fish species is marked with dark stripes or spots, one of them will pass through the eye.

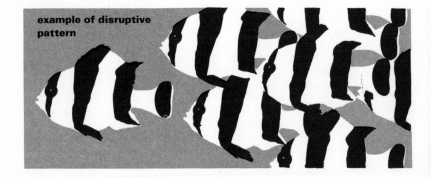

example of disruptive pattern

Eye spots

An eye marking always attracts attention. Therefore, if a fish wishes to be noticed it cannot do better than to emphasize an eye spot (or ocellus). We therefore find a large number of fishes which carry a circular black spot surrounded by white, which gives a fairly good imitation of an eye. There are two points that should be noticed. First, this black spot is always much larger than the true eye, and secondly, it is often positioned on the rear part of the body. The idea is that the enemy which suddenly takes such a fish by surprise will see a black, staring eye so large that it thinks it has to deal with a much larger fish, and also it is completely misled by the position of the eye.

Experiments, with both animals and man, have shown the terrifying effect of such an eye spot, particularly when it is presented suddenly. Such markings are widely distributed in the animal kingdom, particularly in animals which have need of protection, as for example, many of the butterflies.

Poster colours

The beautiful colours of many fishes are very often combined with the principles mentioned above, namely countershading, disruptive pattern and a concealed eye. Sometimes there is a combination of incompatibles, namely of living concealed and yet being as conspicuous as possible to other members of the same species. Thus, during the breeding season – sometimes only during spawning or when the males are actually fighting – the males or both sexes may carry a bright pattern, while at other times they are less conspicuously coloured. Often fishes will show particularly striking areas of the body only when they are needed, for example, by unfolding brilliantly coloured fins, or by raising the gill-covers to reveal the blood-red gills beneath.

Form and colour

Very often the form and colour pattern of a fish are closely linked. Striking colours will be placed on parts of the body which can be displayed to members of the same species. 'Cooperation' between form and colour is even more marked in certain protectively coloured fishes. When a toad-fish resembles a stone covered with algae and a sea-horse is impossible to discern among the seaweeds, one cannot really say whether this is primarily due to their shape or to their colour.

THE RELATIONSHIP OF FISHES

The animals commonly known as fishes really belong to three classes, which are no more closely related to each other than mammals are to birds.

Cyclostomes

These are the last relics of a large group which flourished in former times. This group split off from the line which produced the true fishes some 400–500 million years ago. The only modern representatives are the lampreys and hagfishes, which are not normally kept in aquaria.

Cartilaginous fishes

These are the sharks, dogfishes and rays, which also represent a very old group. The cartilaginous fishes have been more successful in modern times as there are many living species. A few advanced marine aquarists are sometimes successful in keeping small sharks or dogfishes, but none of the species is really suitable for the home aquarium.

Bony fishes

This group contains all the other fishes and of course all of the true aquarium fishes. The family tree on the right shows the relationships of those groups which are of most interest to the aquarist.

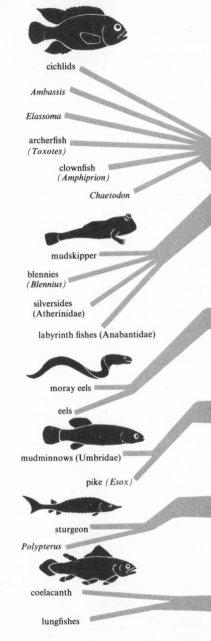

cichlids

Ambassis

Elassoma

archerfish (*Toxotes*)

clownfish (*Amphiprion*)

Chaetodon

mudskipper

blennies (*Blennius*)

silversides (Atherinidae)

labyrinth fishes (Anabantidae)

moray eels

eels

mudminnows (Umbridae)

pike (*Esox*)

sturgeon

Polypterus

coelacanth

lungfishes

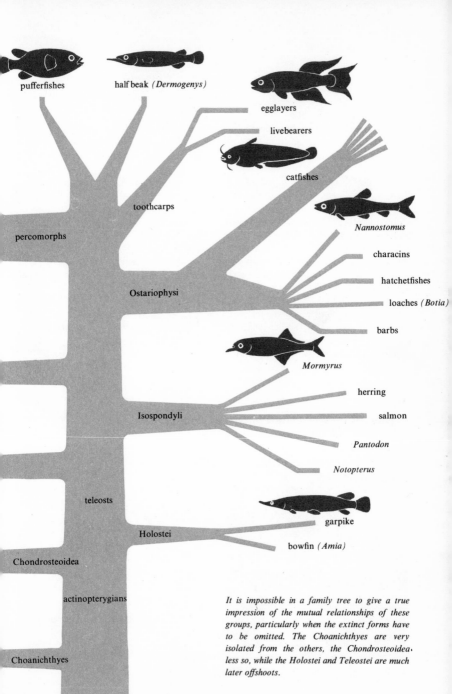

pufferfishes

half beak *(Dermogenys)*

egglayers

livebearers

catfishes

toothcarps

percomorphs

Nannostomus

characins

hatchetfishes

loaches *(Botia)*

barbs

Ostariophysi

Mormyrus

herring

salmon

Pantodon

Isospondyli

Notopterus

teleosts

garpike

bowfin *(Amia)*

Holostei

Chondrosteoidea

actinopterygians

It is impossible in a family tree to give a true impression of the mutual relationships of these groups, particularly when the extinct forms have to be omitted. The Choanichthyes are very isolated from the others, the Chondrosteoidea less so, while the Holostei and Teleostei are much later offshoots.

Choanichthyes

body fishes

14

SPECIES AND SUBSPECIES

The basic unit in systematic biology is known as a species. *Copeina arnoldi* is a species, *Copeina guttata* is another species. In most cases it is implied that all the individuals within a species must resemble each other and be different from those of other species. This rule is, however, subject to certain reservations; one has only to think of the frequent cases of a difference between the sexes, of the differences between domesticated forms, e.g. of the Guppy (p. 92) or of different colour phases (see for example *Aphyosemion gardneri*, p. 80). The important criterion is that, in theory, all the individuals within a species should be capable of breeding with each other and having offspring that are fully fertile in all respects. This has a deeper significance because it allows the free exchange of hereditary characters within the species. If such a free exchange cannot take place, then in the course of time differences will inevitably arise between different populations, which for some reason cannot interbreed, and this will lead to the separation of several species. One can therefore imagine that several species might appear to be so completely alike that they could only be separated by breeding experiments. This is actually known to occur: for example, the different populations of *Aphyosemion bivittatum* (p. 82) which resemble each other but cannot interbreed, must be regarded as separate species. When a species is divided into separate populations, as for example when it inhabits different river systems or lives on separated islands, it often happens that differences arise between these populations, even though they will still interbreed. Different populations of this kind are termed subspecies or geographical races.

Several closely related species are combined into a genus, several closely related genera into a family and several related families into an order.

Example of the distribution of two subspecies of Barbus tetrazona

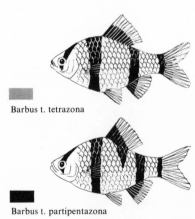

Barbus t. tetrazona

Barbus t. partipentazona

FISH NAMES

Every kind of fish – like all other living organisms – has a Latin or scientific name consisting of a generic (genus) name and a specific (species) name. *Barbus tetrazona* belongs to the genus *Barbus*, which contains several other species. This species is divided into several subspecies, such as *Barbus tetrazona tetrazona* and *Barbus tetrazona partipentazona*. Sometimes the name is written as: *Barbus tetrazona* (Bleeker 1855). This denotes that the species concerned was first described by the zoologist Bleeker in 1855, and when his name stands in parenthesis it means that he described it under a different generic name (actually under *Puntius* instead of *Barbus*), but that the species was later transferred to the genus *Barbus*. If he had described it under the generic and specific name in use today his name would not have stood in parenthesis. This use of the author's name and year is really only appropriate in purely scientific works and, since the aquarist will normally never wish to refer to the original descriptions these have been omitted from this book.

But why do most aquarists use the scientific names instead of the popular common names? A name must characterize an animal or an object as precisely as possible. This the popular names do not always do. So many fishes are imported that many of them are distributed by the trade without a popular name or with chance names which do not find favour. Many fish species have different common names in different countries or even in different regions of the same country. The scientific name has the great advantage of being precise, for such names are only given under very strict international rules which are respected in all parts of the world.

There are two very important rules in giving scientific names. One is that the first time a name is given in the scientific literature, it must refer to a so-called type specimen – the holotype – a specimen of the new species that is clearly marked and deposited in an official and accessible collection, usually in a museum or laboratory. It is then possible at a future date to visit the museum concerned, examine the type specimen and compare it with one's own fish and so decide whether the latter belongs to the same species or to a different one. The other important rule is the so-called rule of priority, according to which the first properly published specific name of a fish is the correct one. If, therefore, a fish has once been described under a given name, a later worker cannot give it another name nor can he use this name for another fish.

This system is not quite so perfect in practice as it is in theory, because it is often difficult to decide with certainty whether a species in the hand is identical to or different from a faded preserved specimen in a museum. One can make a mistake and thus allow a new fish to go under an old name or describe a known species under a new name. Another source of error is that one can easily overlook an old paper in which a species has been described and thus give a new description to the species concerned. When the mistake is noticed – sometimes after many years – the first published name must be used.

It may happen that a research worker divides a genus, so that some of its species are given a new generic name. In such a case the original generic name is used for the group of species to which the first described species belongs.

Examples of changes in the names of aquarium fishes are given on pages 60 and 80.

DISTRIBUTION OF FISHES

No single species of fish is found in all parts of the world. Fishes have only a limited capacity to spread from one area to another. Freshwater fishes can seldom if ever cross stretches of sea, and differences in water type often have a similar restricting effect. By studying the distribution of the various groups it is possible to form an idea of what the earth looked like in earlier geological periods, what land connections existed and which areas were isolated for long periods, and also, which groups of fishes are old and which younger.

A group such as the lungfishes today has 5 species which are widely separated in space. We must assume that at one time the lungfishes were distributed over the whole of the world and this is, in fact, supported by fossil evidence. This group is now in retreat, and may be dying out.

In contrast, the cichlids are a 'modern' family with about 1000 species in South America and tropical Africa, but only two in southern Asia, where in other respects the conditions would be good for them. There is still considerable discussion about how the dispersal took place between South America and Africa. In the following pages the distribution of each species is given. This is of interest to the aquarist, for it gives him a rough idea of the conditions under which the fish lives in the wild state. In many cases the distribution given is very approximate. It often happens that a species is only known from a few localities, its total range being unknown, and sometimes the commercial collector keeps the place of capture secret in order to conceal it from competitors. Nothing can be done about this, for animal collectors must earn a living, and they therefore have a right to preserve their trade secrets.

It must also be emphasized that no fish will occur in all the rivers and lakes within its geographical range. Every fish requires certain well-defined conditions of temperature, light, current, type of water, etc., and this means that it will only occur in habitats where these requirements are fulfilled, and the more rigorous the requirements, the more restricted will be its distribution. One could therefore have two species sharing the same broad geographical distribution, without ever finding them in the same river, because they require different environmental conditions; this is something aquarists should think about when setting up aquaria arranged on a geographical basis. Normally the natural conditions in the same habitat in different parts of the world will be much more uniform than conditions in different habitats in the same locality. A fish living in a slow-flowing forest stream in Africa will therefore have much more in common with species living in the same type of stream in South America than with a fish from a different habitat in Africa, even though this may be only a few miles away.

FRESHWATER FISHES

The great majority of aquarists are concerned with freshwater fishes – only a few keep the more difficult marine species – and almost all the aquarist's freshwater fishes come from the tropics. Here one finds the most brilliantly coloured species, and in many ways it is easier to keep tropical fishes in an aquarium than cold-water species, which may require a great amount of oxygen and may be uncomfortable in the temperatures found in a living room.

The aquarist's fishes come from all parts of the tropics. Every year more and more aquarium fishes appear on the market in an attempt to satisfy the enormous demands of millions of aquarists, especially in Europe and North America. Of the numerous new species imported every year most quickly disappear again, because they are too difficult to keep, not attractive enough, or because their place of capture is too remote for collecting to be a feasible economic proposition, but a few remain. From these few we have, over the years, built up the relatively constant repertoire of classical aquarium fishes which are presented in this book.

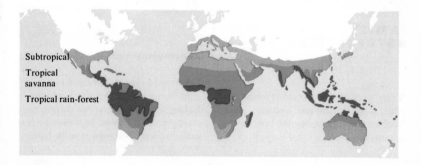

Subtropical

Tropical savanna

Tropical rain-forest

FAMILY PANTODONTIDAE

This family contains only the following species.

Pantodon buchholzi

BUTTERFLY FISH

Tropical West Africa from Nigeria to the Congo, in the rain-forest region: 5 in.

The butterfly fish is a typical surface-living fish. In nature and in the aquarium it can be seen hanging motionless among the vegetation. As soon as an insect approaches the surface, or falls down on to it, the fish advances in a flash and snaps it up in its enormous, upward-directed mouth. This is a hardy species, but difficult to breed. It prefers soft, slightly acid peat-moss water. Part of its diet should consist of flies, grasshoppers and the like, and it gives most pleasure when kept in a tank with shallow water so that it can be observed from above as well as from the side.

Notopterus afer

Africa from Gambia to the Congo; 24 in.

Young specimens of this and related species are imported from time to time and their unusual behaviour attracts the attention of aquarists. They live among dense vegetation or below an overhanging branch, where a small school of them will often remain closely packed together. Now and again they make short excursions out into the tank and one can then see that they swim backwards as well as forwards by the undulating movement of the anal fin. At night these fish leave their hiding-place and swim around. Since they are shy of the light, their tank should be provided with dark hiding places; otherwise they will not do well. They are best fed on live food of the appropriate size and they prefer soft, slightly acid water and temperatures in the low 80's F.

Only the young have the marbled pattern and they later become uniform in colour and far less attractive.

Notopterus afer

FAMILY NOTOPTERIDAE

KNIFEFISHES

A very small family of peculiar freshwater fishes from Africa and southern Asia. None of the species has yet bred in the aquarium.

Xenomystus nigri

Central and western Africa; 8 in.

In this species the dorsal fin is completely lacking and the ventral fins have almost disappeared. It can be kept like the preceding species, but appears to be hardier.

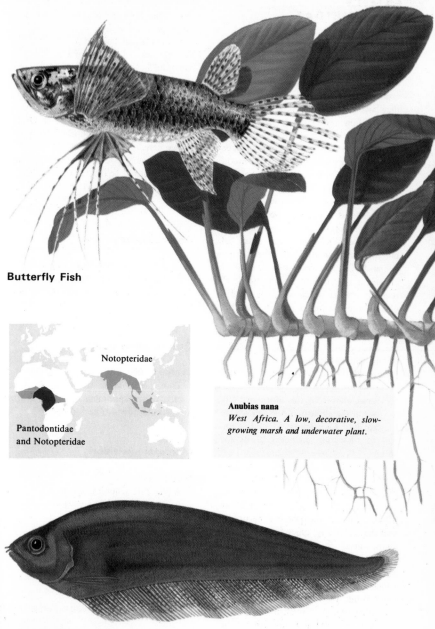

Butterfly Fish

Notopteridae

Pantodontidae
and Notopteridae

Anubias nana
West Africa. A low, decorative, slow-growing marsh and underwater plant.

Xenomystus nigri

FAMILY MORMYRIDAE

A small family only represented in the fresh waters of Africa. Several of the smaller species are imported from time to time, but none can be said to have become established as aquarium fishes, because they have never been bred. The mormyrids have certain very special characteristics which make them extremely interesting for those who wish to make an effort to keep them. All the species live either in muddy water or dimly lit locations, and they have developed a characteristic system of orientation which is only known in a few other fishes. This is a series of electric organs which are not strong enough to give a shock capable of paralysing other fish, but are used exclusively for orientation. When the fish releases impulses, it sets up around it a system of electric fields, the relative form of which will be altered by objects in the vicinity of the fish. Along the sides of the body the mormyrids have sense organs which can detect these changes in the electric field, and thus the fish can obtain what is probably a very accurate picture of the objects, living and dead, in its vicinity. These electric pulses can be measured and from the mormyrid's behaviour in the aquarium one can see that they are used, for example, for finding food and for detecting members of its own species.

Presumably because of the complicated central nervous system necessary to sort out these electric impulses the mormyrids have relatively the largest brain of any fishes. This has the peculiar by-product that they are always quick to learn and can show varied forms of behaviour. For example, many of the species are known to play with pieces of twig or similar objects which they balance on the snout as they move round the aquarium. Some species are rather aggressive towards their fellows although peaceful towards other fishes. The electric systems presumably disturb each other, so it is best not to keep several individuals in the same tank, even if each one is provided with its own hiding-place.

Mormyrids are best fed with worms of a suitable size which burrow in the soft substrate, but some species gradually learn to take dead food on the bottom. These fishes should preferably be kept in soft, slightly acid water, but they are not very sensitive to the quality of the water. Of the relatively few species imported, three are shown here.

The systematics of this family are not fully understood, so the names used should be treated with a certain amount of reserve.

Gnathonemus petersi

West Africa from Niger to Congo; 9 in.
A peaceful species with a long, mobile snout which it uses for rooting in soft bottoms.

Gnathonemus schilthuisi

Central Congo; 2 in.
This species lacks the long, sensitive snout. Young specimens of the same size are peaceful towards each other.

Marcusenius isidori

Eastern Africa; 4 in.
A peaceful, schooling species.

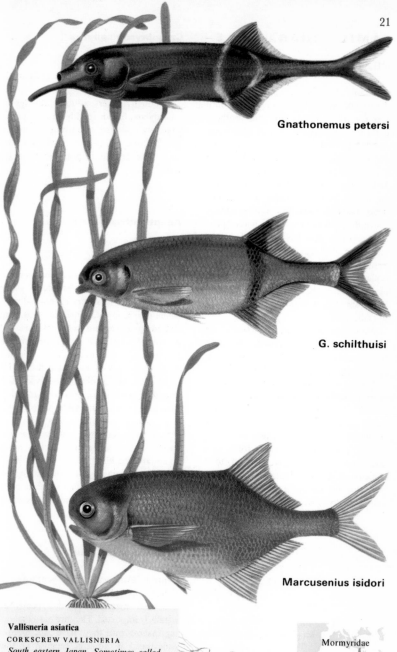

Gnathonemus petersi

G. schilthuisi

Marcusenius isidori

Vallisneria asiatica
CORKSCREW VALLISNERIA
South eastern Japan. Sometimes called
V. spiralis *f.* tortifolia.

Mormyridae

FAMILY CHARACIDAE

CHARACINS

A family with many species, mainly distributed in the fresh waters of South and Central America and the southern parts of North America, but with some species in Central Africa. This peculiar distribution has been cited as an argument in favour of the theory that South America and Africa were joined until fairly recent geological times, but there is much evidence that the characins were originally distributed throughout Africa and tropical Asia and that they have spread from the latter area to North America and later to South America. The group was then replaced in Asia by other families. Characins never have barbels, but they usually have a small, rayless adipose fin behind the dorsal fin.

With a few exceptions the characins are small, peaceful and usually colourful fishes, many species of which have therefore become popular among aquarists.

The exceptions to peacefulness are the piranhas in the genera *Serrasalmus, Rooseveltiella* and *Pygocentrus*. These fishes are well-known for the violence with which they hunt in schools and tear swimming animals apart with their sharp teeth; even large mammals may be reduced to a skeleton in a few minutes. Piranhas are imported into Europe and North America from time to time.

Ctenobrycon spilurus

SILVER TETRA

Northern South America, in coastal districts; 3 in.

Although not very colourful this species is hardy and breeds readily when kept in a large, well-planted aquarium. It prefers 70–82°F, but will tolerate lower temperatures. The female is plumper than the male.

Anoptichthys jordani

BLIND CAVE-FISH

Caves in Mexico; 3 in.

This fish, which was first discovered in 1936, is found in subterranean watercourses in a few limestone caves in Mexico, where it lives in total darkness. It is blind and unpigmented, but its lateral line is well developed so that it can detect minute changes in pressure and thus orientate itself nearly as well as sighted fishes. The blind cave-fish probably evolved from *Astyanax mexicanus*, which is found in surface waters in the same areas, but is now so different that it has even been placed in a different genus. The two species are no longer able to interbreed. In aquaria the blind cave-fish is extremely hardy and manages just as well as sighted fishes, but is best kept in a separate dimly lit tank with hard water and no vegetation.

Astyanax mexicanus

Central America and south-western U.S.A.; up to 6 in.

Several members of this genus are regularly imported. They are hardy schooling fishes, but they have not become widespread in aquaria because of their relatively large size and unspectacular coloration.

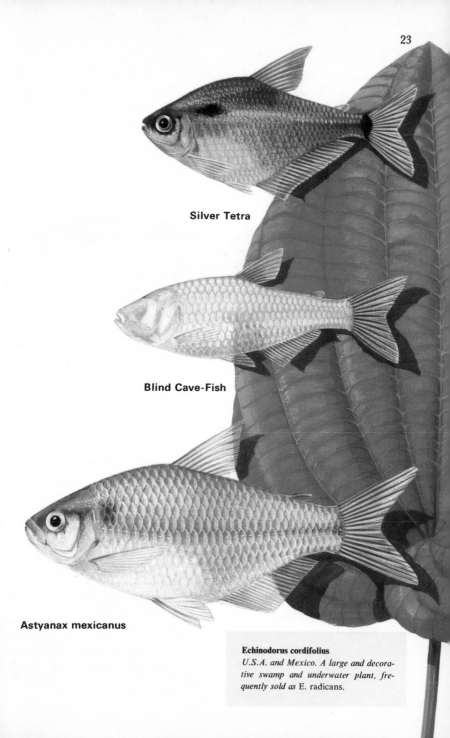

23

Silver Tetra

Blind Cave-Fish

Astyanax mexicanus

Echinodorus cordifolius
U.S.A. and Mexico. A large and decorative swamp and underwater plant, frequently sold as E. radicans.

Moenkhausia pittieri

Glass Tetra

Moenkhausia pittieri

Venezuela; up to 2 in.

A distinctive aquarium fish with long fins and shining scales. The female is duller than the male and has a shorter dorsal fin. This species is best kept in soft, slightly acid water.

Moenkhausia oligolepis

GLASS TETRA

Amazon and Guyana, in standing or sluggish waters; 5 in.

A rather large fish, best suited to the large community tank and quite easy to breed. In the female the fins, especially the anal, are shorter than in the male.

A similar species, *M. sanctae-filomenae*, is imported from Paraguay. It only reaches a length of 2½ in. and has a somewhat deeper body.

Megalamphodus megalopterus

Matto Grosso, Brazil; 1¾ in.

A recently imported, beautiful tetra which has proved to be robust. It seems to prefer soft, slightly acid water for spawning. This species shows marked sexual dimorphism: the male is very dark grey with long fins, while the female is red with shorter fins.

Black Tetra

young fish

Gymnocorymbus ternetzi

BLACK TETRA

Rio Paraguay, South America; 2 in.

A very quiet and peaceful aquarium fish, which is also suitable for smaller tanks. The beautiful nearly black rear half of the body seen in young fish unfortunately fades with age, so the adults are less striking. Easily bred at 80–82°F.

♂ ♀

Megalamphodus megalopterus

Megalamphodus sweglesi

Upper Amazon; up to 1½ in.

Although this little tetra was only found in 1960 and named in 1961 it has already become widespread. There are no problems in keeping this species but breeding still seems to be very difficult. It is best attempted in soft water with a small amount of added salt, and the lighting should be subdued. The male has a pointed dorsal fin without the dark marking.

♀

Megalamphodus sweglesi

Elodea densa
South America to Florida. A very hardy water plant that will grow without being rooted.

Corynopoma riisei

SWORDTAIL CHARACIN

Trinidad and northern Venezuela; 3 in.

The male has very elongated fins and also a peculiar long appendage on the gill-cover. This appendage is thickened at the end and is usually carried close to the body, but during mating it sticks out at right angles to the body and the male strokes the female with it. It is probable that the female regards the appendage as food, for she is attracted to it. When this happens the male manages to reach the side of the female. The normal method of fertilization among characins, where the male simply releases the sperm at the same time as the female lays the eggs, does not apply to the swordtail characin; here the sperm are enclosed in a sperm capsule (spermatophore) which is inserted into the oviduct of the female, where it is stored until the female lays the eggs; the actual laying may be delayed for some time. It appears that a single mating provides the female with enough sperm to last her lifetime. The eggs hatch after 20–36 hours and the young are easy to rear.

It is a pity that this easily contented species is so seldom seen in aquaria. Besides the greyish-green natural form, a white form occurs in aquaria.

Pseudocorynopoma doriae

DRAGON-FINNED CHARACIN

South Brazil and La Plata district; 3 in.

This species is very closely related to *C. riisei*, and mating occurs in the same curious fashion. In this species, however, the male has no appendage on the gill-cover, but in contrast to the female has greatly elongated fins. It thrives best at rather low temperatures, 60–64°F, and is extremely robust and peaceful.

Copeina arnoldi

SPRAYING CHARACIN

Lower Amazon, Rio Para; ♂ 3 in., ♀ 2 in.

A peaceful, hardy and elegant surface fish which has the strange habit of depositing its eggs out of the water. During mating both fishes spring up onto leaves of plants, plant stems or, in aquaria, the cover-glass. The female deposits a few eggs there which immediately adhere. These 'hops' are repeated until a few hundred eggs have been laid. After spawning the male guards the eggs, something quite unique among the characins, spraying them with water with his caudal fin so that they remain moist. After 27–36 hours the eggs hatch and the young fall into the water. The parents should now be removed. The young are very small and need extremely fine live food. Breeding this species is often difficult. The water should be soft and slightly acid and the tank should be large and planted with a few large-leaved plants.

Copeina guttata

RED-SPOTTED COPEINA

Central Amazon region; 6 in.

A large and less attractive species which is rarely seen in aquaria. This species is very prolific and spawns readily, the eggs being deposited in a pit in the aquarium sand. The female is paler than the male and lacks the prolongation of the upper lobe of the caudal fin.

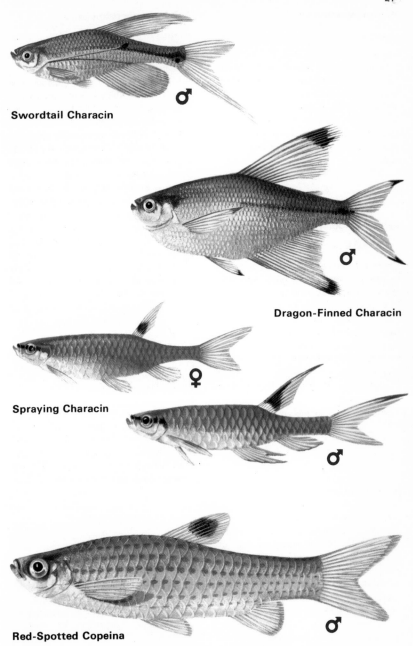

Swordtail Characin

Dragon-Finned Characin

Spraying Characin

♀

♂

Red-Spotted Copeina

Pyrrhulina vittata

STRIPED VITTATA

Amazon region; 2 in.

Several different species of *Pyrrhulina* are imported from time to time but they have not become very widespread. They are rather delicate, peaceful surface-living fish, closely related to *Copeina*. The eggs are deposited on large leaves which have previously been carefully cleaned by the male.

Pristella riddlei

X-RAY FISH or PRISTELLA

Venezuela, Guyana and lower Amazon, in brooks and small rivers, often with little water; ♂ 1 in., ♀ 1¾ in.

A fast-moving hardy species which even thrives in hard water. Not every sexually mature male and female will make up a mating pair and the fish should be allowed to choose for themselves. The young are very small and need the finest live food and a large tank, as the broods are often numerous (up to three or four hundred). The female is larger and heavier than the male.

Hasemania marginata

South-eastern Brazil; 1½ in.

A very beautiful and undemanding aquarium fish which should be kept at 68–75°F; it spawns readily, preferably at 75°F. After spawning, the parents should be removed and the tank darkened. The eggs hatch in 24 hours, and the young hang from plants or the glass for three or four days; they should be fed with infusorians or sieved hard-boiled egg yolk. The female is larger and paler than the male.

Aphyocharax rubripinnis

BLOODFIN

Lower Rio La Plata, around Ozario, in Argentina; 1¾ in.

A beautiful, lively and undemanding schooling fish which is very suitable for the beginner. It should be kept in a large tank, preferably at 68–77°F. There is no difference in colour between the sexes, but the male is usually slimmer than the female and its anal and ventral fins have small hooks on them.

Easily bred in soft to medium-hard water. The numerous eggs are glass-clear and small. The parents will eat the eggs; so the bottom of the tank should have a grid or a layer of stones. The eggs hatch in 24 hours at 75–79°F, and the fry then hang for three to four days. They will readily eat infusorians, dried food or egg yolk, and they grow very rapidly.

Alestes longipinnis

LONG-FINNED CHARACIN

West Africa, in swiftly flowing waters; 5 in.

Several species of the genus *Alestes* are imported, but they have not yet become very widespread because of their size and relatively dull coloration. Hardy and lively fishes for the large aquarium. The male has an elongated dorsal fin.

Lagarosiphon muscoides
South Africa. Sold as Elodea crispa. *Requires plenty of light and a rather low temperature. Can grow without being rooted.*

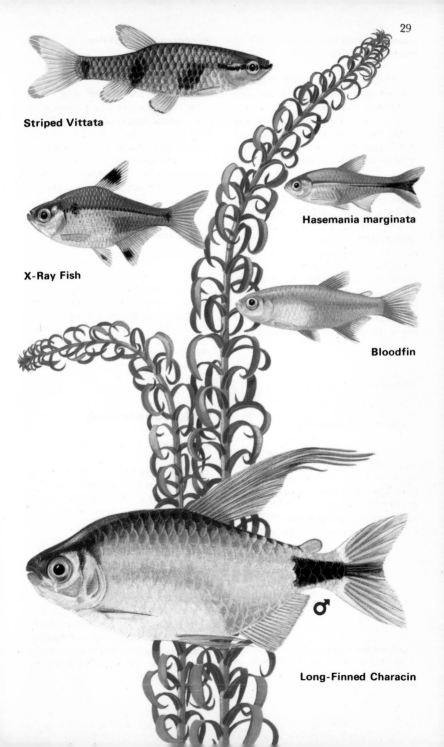

Striped Vittata

Hasemania marginata

X-Ray Fish

Bloodfin

♂

Long-Finned Characin

Hemigrammus and Hyphessobrycon

Two Central and South American genera, very rich in species, which contain some of the most beautiful and most popular aquarium fishes. These two genera are very closely related, the only difference being that *Hemigrammus* has scales at the base of the caudal fin but *Hyphessobrycon* does not.

Many species of *Hemigrammus* and *Hyphessobrycon* show no clear sexual dimorphism, though the female is usually stouter than the male. An apparently constant difference can be observed, however, when the fish are viewed by transmitted light. The swim bladder of the male is more tapered posteriorly than that of the female, and in the male there is usually a free space between the swim bladder and the other internal organs, whereas in the female this space is occupied by the ovary.

Hemigrammus caudovittatus

BUENOS AIRES TETRA

La Plata region, Argentina; 3 in.

The female is plumper than the male and has almost colourless fins. This species breeds readily at 75°F in soft, slightly acid water, preferably filtered through peat. Morning sunshine on the aquarium, which should be richly furnished with fine-leaved plants, encourages spawning. *H. caudovittatus* sometimes eats plants with soft leaves.

Echinodorus longistylis
Brazil. Requires rich soil, soft water and plenty of light.

Hemigrammus ocellifer

BEACON FISH OR HEAD-AND-TAIL LIGHT TETRA

Amazon Basin and Guyana; 1¾ in.

The bright marking is supposed to show that in nature this fish inhabits small, dark pools in the rain-forest. In such surroundings the iridescent spot guides members of the same species to the position of the school. Can be bred without difficulty, even in hard water, and is very prolific.

Hemigrammus pulcher

PRETTY TETRA

Upper Amazon area; 2 in.

An exceptionally beautiful fish, which, like the previous species, inhabits dark forest waters. It is more difficult to breed than the other species of *Hemigrammus*, even in soft, acid water. The young eat only the finest live food and grow slowly. Temperature 77–82 °F.

Hemigrammus hyanuary

Lake Hyanuary on the Rio Negro, Brazil; 1½ in.

A recently imported species that has not yet become very widespread. This is a difficult fish to breed; it usually spawns in the late afternoon or, in artificial lighting, in the evening.

Hemigrammus armstrongi

GOLDEN TETRA

Western Guyana; 1¾ in.

An attractive species which usually spawns readily. Unfortunately the golden iridescence disappears in young hatched in the aquarium. This is possibly caused by an inadequate diet.

Buenos Aires Tetra

Beacon Fish

Pretty Tetra

H. hyanuary

Golden Tetra

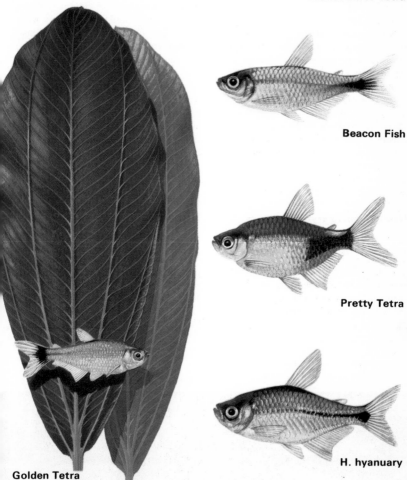

Hemigrammus rhodostomus

RED-NOSED OR RUMMY-NOSED TETRA

Lower Amazon; 1½ in.

The intensive red colour on the head disappears if the fish are not in good condition. This species is very difficult to breed.

Hemigrammus nanus

SILVER-TIPPED TETRA

Rio San Francisco, eastern Brazil; 2 in.

A hardy species that should be kept in the same way as the other species of *Hemigrammus*. Outside the breeding season both sexes are silvery-grey to yellowish with a dark longitudinal band and a spot at the base of the caudal fin. In the breeding season the male becomes a very attractive brownish-red. In recent years an American breeder has had a form in which both sexes show this red coloration throughout the year. This colour variant is the one illustrated here.

Hemigrammus erythrozonus

GLOWLIGHT TETRA

Guyana; 1½ in.

Perhaps the most popular and widespread species of *Hemigrammus*, it was formerly known as *Hyphessobrycon gracilis*. A hardy fish which should be kept in soft, moderately acid water. It usually spawns at about 82°F.

Hyphessobrycon flammeus

FLAME TETRA

Rio de Janeiro district; 1¾ in.

One of the earliest imported and most beautiful species of *Hyphessobrycon*, which has now unfortunately been superseded by other more colourful species. This is a pity, as besides being exceptionally attractive it is also hardy and spawns more readily then other members of the genus; it can even be bred in fairly hard water. The eggs hatch in two or three days and the young hang from plants for three or four days. They should then be fed with fine live food. A small school of this tetra would adorn any community aquarium and should not be lacking in the beginner's tank. The males can be very quarrelsome, but probably cannot harm each other seriously. In the male the anal fin has a dark edge.

Hyphessobrycon griemi

GRIEM'S TETRA

Brazil; 1 in.

Very similar to *Hyphessobrycon flammeus* to which it may be closely related, but the red colour is somewhat less vivid. This species is very rarely imported.

Glowlight tetras as seen in a dark rain-forest.

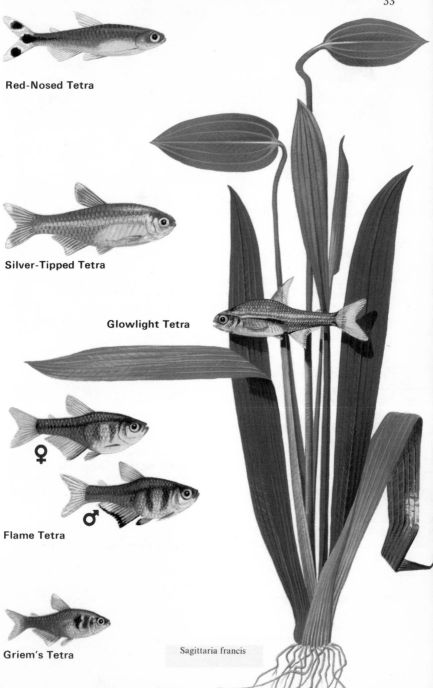

Red-Nosed Tetra

Silver-Tipped Tetra

Glowlight Tetra

♀

♂

Flame Tetra

Griem's Tetra

Sagittaria francis

Hyphessobrycon 'roberti'

Hyphessobrycon 'roberti'

An attractive species that has not yet been given a proper scientific name; H. 'roberti' is only a trade name. It is possibly very closely related to the true *Hyphessobrycon rosaceus*.

elongated dorsal fin. There are various races which vary considerably in colour, the most popular being the deep red forms. This species can be bred without great difficulty.

Hyphessobrycon ornatus

Upper Amazon, Guyana; 1½ in.

An exceptionally beautiful fish which is much in demand. It is easy to keep but difficult to breed. It is frequently imported, usually under the name *H. rosaceus*, but the genuine *H. rosaceus* is very rarely imported. Both of these species can be distinguished from the other 'Rosy Tetras' by the absence of the shoulder blotch. The two species can be distinguished from each other by the absence of the red caudal spot and the elongated dorsal fin in the male of *H. rosaceus*.

Hyphessobrycon serpae

Central Amazon Basin; 1¾ in.

This species has an indistinct shoulder blotch and the male does not have an

Hyphessobrycon callistus

JEWEL TETRA

Rio Paraguay and Matto Grosso; 1 in.

This 'rosy tetra' is characterized by a very well-developed shoulder blotch. It is seldom imported. All the 'rosy tetras' mentioned on this page, plus a few rarely imported ones *(H. bentosi, H. minor, H. copelandi)* are sometimes regarded as subspecies of *H. callistus*.

Hyphessobrycon rubrostigma

BLEEDING HEART TETRA

Colombia; 3 in.

This is the largest representative of the 'rosy tetra' group and is characterized by the blood-red spot on the flank. Breeding is difficult. A dark vertical streak runs across the eye.

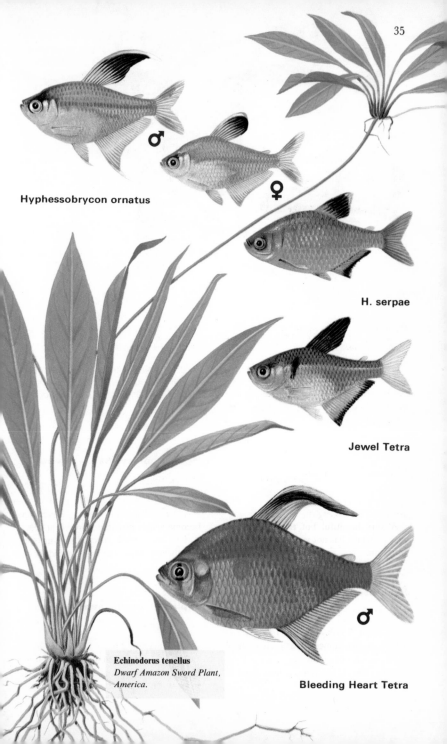

Hyphessobrycon ornatus

♂

♀

H. serpae

Jewel Tetra

Echinodorus tenellus
*Dwarf Amazon Sword Plant,
America.*

♂

Bleeding Heart Tetra

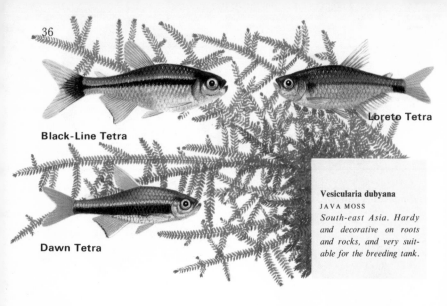

Black-Line Tetra

Loreto Tetra

Dawn Tetra

Vesicularia dubyana
JAVA MOSS
*South-east Asia. Hardy
and decorative on roots
and rocks, and very suit-
able for the breeding tank.*

Hyphessobrycon scholzei

BLACK-LINE TETRA

Amazon Basin; 2 in.

This tetra is not particularly colourful, but is very easy to breed. The young feed on infusorians for the first few days, after which they should be given newly-hatched brine shrimp or very fine dried food.

Hyphessobrycon eos

DAWN TETRA

Western Guyana; 1¾ in.

A very beautiful but rarely imported species, which has not yet been bred in the aquarium.

Hyphessobrycon metae

LORETO TETRA

Meta River, South America; 1¾ in.

One of the numerous attractive small tetras which appear on the market from time to time. It has not yet been bred in the aquarium.

Hyphessobrycon pulchripinnis

LEMON TETRA

Amazon Basin; 2 in.

A popular species which is not easy to breed. In the female the anal fin lacks the black margin.

Hyphessobrycon herbertaxelrodi

BLACK NEON

Rio Taquari, Amazon Basin; 1¼ in.

A very beautiful species which has become widely distributed in recent years. It has been bred successfully in soft, slightly acid water, but this is still difficult.

Hyphessobrycon heterorhabdus

FLAG TETRA

Lower Amazon; 2 in.

A widely distributed and rather delicate species which requires soft, slightly acid water if it is to thrive.

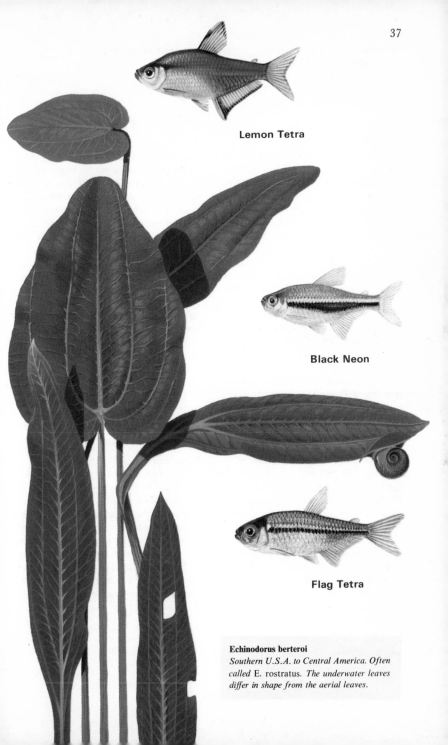

Lemon Tetra

Black Neon

Flag Tetra

Echinodorus berteroi
Southern U.S.A. to Central America. Often called E. rostratus. *The underwater leaves differ in shape from the aerial leaves.*

Paracheirodon innesi
(or Hyphessobrycon innesi)

NEON TETRA

Small streams of the Upper Amazon Basin;
1½ in.

Because of its magnificent colours this
fish attracted much attention when it was
imported in the 1930s. Its iridescence
indicates that the Neon Tetra lives in the
dark waters of the rain-forest. At that time
it was sold at a high price as importation
was difficult and for a long time the species
withstood all efforts to breed it in aquaria.
Since then it has been bred successfully in
many places, so that it is no longer regarded
as a problem fish, though it is by no means
one of the easiest fishes to breed. It is also
imported into some countries from South-
east Asia where it is bred out of doors, and
this has kept the price quite low.

The neon tetra is very hardy and robust,
thrives in every type of water, even at quite
low temperatures and is not fastidious
about food.

In contrast to its hardiness, it is difficult
to breed. This seems primarily to be a
question of giving it the right type of
water. Breeding has been much easier
since the value of the so-called rain-forest
water, i.e. almost calcium-free and slightly
acid, has been learned. It seems to be
important that the female should be mated
as soon as she is old enough to do so, and
the temperature must not be too high (not
above 75°F). When the young are hatched,
they appear to thrive best in rather harder
water than that in which they were born.
There is no marked difference between the
sexes, but the female is more robust than
the male, and has a more rounded belly
profile.

Cheirodon axelrodi

CARDINAL TETRA

Rio Negro; 2 in.

Sometimes called *Hyphessobrycon cardinalis*, a name which was, however,
published one day later than the name
C. axelrodi, and is therefore invalid,
according to the rules of priority.

The introduction in 1956 of a neon-type
fish even more magnificent than the well-
known *Paracheirodon innesi* created quite
a sensation. The cardinal tetra must surely
be the most brilliantly coloured of all
fresh-water fishes, with its glowing reds
and blues.

This species is also difficult to breed. It
seems to prefer a higher breeding temperature than *P. innesi* (about 77–81°F), and
usually spawns in the evening. The young
grow very slowly. In other respects the
species is even hardier than the neon tetra
and is not susceptible to *Plistophora* (see
page 198). There appear to be different
populations with different maximum sizes.

Arnoldichthys spilopterus

RED-EYED CHARACIN

Nigeria; 3 in.

This exceptionally attractive West African characin is rarely seen. It is difficult
to keep, requiring soft, slightly acid water
and a dark aquarium with dense clumps
of plants and plenty of space for swimming. It has so far never been bred in the
aquarium, although it should be no more
difficult than the other rain-forest fishes.
The male can be distinguished from the
female by its very convex anal fin.

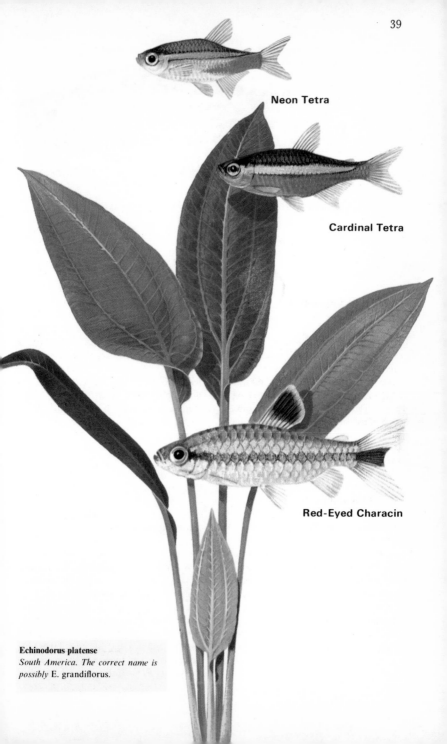

Neon Tetra

Cardinal Tetra

Red-Eyed Characin

Echinodorus platense
South America. The correct name is possibly E. grandiflorus.

♂

Congo Tetra

Micralestes interruptus

CONGO TETRA

Congo Basin; 3 in.

A magnificent fish which is only seen at its best when kept in a large tank. The female is slightly smaller than the male and does not have the beautifully elongated fins. The Congo Tetra is quite robust and prefers soft water and a fairly high temperature (about 77°F). It is difficult to breed, although this has been done in the aquarium.

Thayeria boehlkei

Upper Amazon Basin (Marañon River); 3 in.

In Europe this species is usually sold under the name *T. obliquua,* in the U.S.A. as *T. sanctae-mariae*. A few specimens of the genuine *T. obliquua* have only recently been imported (and to make the confusion complete these are sold in some places as *T. sanctae-mariae*). A third member of the genus, *T. ifati*, is rarely imported.

T. boehlkei is a hardy species that is not difficult to breed.

Nematobrycon palmeri

West slope of Colombian Andes; 2 in.

A fine species in which the old males may be almost black on the flanks with very elongated tips to the caudal fins. The female is paler and lacks the elongated fins. Unlike most other tetras, *N. palmeri* is not a schooling fish. It is a quiet, fairly hardy, bottom-living species, which is rather difficult to breed, even in soft, acid water.

Exodon paradoxus

North-eastern South America; 6 in.

A very beautiful species which cannot, however, be readily recommended as an aquarium fish. It grows very large, is extremely aggressive even towards species larger than itself and can damage other fishes with its sharp teeth. It must, therefore, be kept in a separate tank. It has only been bred a few times and the rearing of the young seems to be extremely difficult.

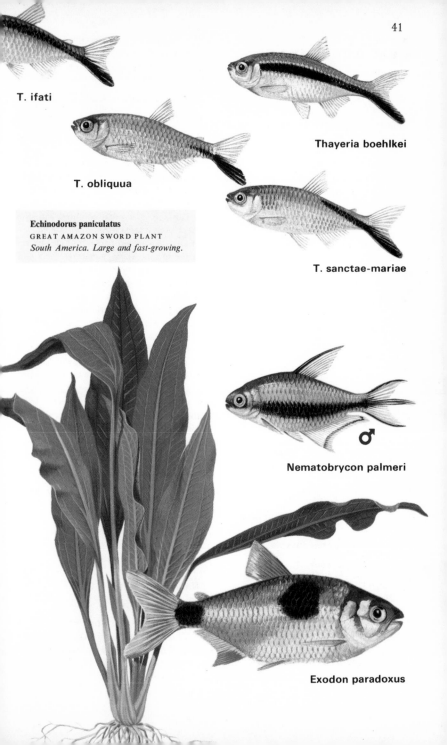

T. ifati

Thayeria boehlkei

T. obliquua

Echinodorus paniculatus
GREAT AMAZON SWORD PLANT
South America. Large and fast-growing.

T. sanctae-mariae

Nematobrycon palmeri

Exodon paradoxus

FAMILY HEMIODONTIDAE

A small South American family, previously included among the characins, but now separated from them because of the toothless lower jaw. They have very small mouths which can make feeding difficult and many species only eat the finer types of live food. The water temperature should be in the range 77–82°F.

The young are very small and must be fed with extremely fine live food, such as brine shrimp, nauplii or rotifers. They grow rather slowly.

The remarkable colour change that takes place during the course of twenty-four hours seems to be common to all the *Nannostomus* species. During the day they have conspicuous longitudinal bands, but at night many species carry transverse bars.

Nannostomus marginatus

DWARF PENCILFISH

Surinam and Guyana; 1½ in.

The sexes can be distinguished by the shape of the anal fin, that of the male being rounded, that of the female being straight posteriorly. It is possible that this sexual difference applies to all species of *Nannostomus*. This species breeds in soft, slightly acid water, but the parents devour their freshly-spawned eggs if they possibly can; so the breeding tank must be densely planted with fine-leaved plants.

Nannostomus aripirangensis

GOLDEN PENCILFISH

Aripiranga Island in the lower Amazon; 1½ in.

A very beautiful *Nannostomus* species, the male in particular being quite magnificent when ready to mate; the female is much paler.

This species is often confused with the very closely related *Nannostomus anomalus*. In fact they are probably both subspecies of the species *Nannostomus beckfordi* and the situation is further complicated by the fact that most specimens seen in aquaria under the name *N. aripirangensis* are hybrids between this form and *N. anomalus*, and that the genuine *N. aripirangensis* is perhaps not imported at all.

N. aripirangensis can be distinguished from *N. anomalus* by the following characters: (1) The red stripe over the golden longitudinal band is continuous and brightly coloured, (2) A fine red line runs from the insertion of the pectoral fin to the anal fin, (3) The ventral fins are blood-red with bluish tips, (4) During mating the caudal peduncle (base of the tail) of the male is blood-red.

Nannostomus harrisoni

West Guyana; 2½ in.

A rare, large and beautiful *Nannostomus* species, which has very seldom bred successfully in the aquarium.

Nannostomus trifasciatus

THREE-STRIPED PENCILFISH

West Guyana and Central Amazon; 2½ in.

This species should be kept in the same way as the other *Nannostomus* species, but breeding appears to be difficult. The female is more rounded and paler than the male.

Dwarf Pencilfish

Golden Pencilfish

N. harrisoni

Three-Striped Pencilfish

Hygrophilia polysperma
South Asia. Hardy and fast-growing.

Nannostomus eques

TUBE-MOUTHED PENCILFISH

Middle Amazon and Guyana; 2 in.

This is a typical species of *Nannostomus* as regards care and behaviour, except that its normal swimming position is very oblique, sometimes vertical, with the head upwards. The significance of this is not clear, but perhaps it allows the fish to hide more easily between the sloping or vertical leaves of water plants. Hardy and spawns readily.

FAMILY ANOSTOMIDAE

A small South American family, some of whose members have become very widespread as aquarium fishes.

Anostomus anostomus

STRIPED ANOSTOMUS OR
HEADSTANDER

Guyana and Amazon Basin; 6 in.

A very beautiful but unfortunately rather large species which swims in an oblique position with the head down. With its small mouth it browses among vegetation, stones, fallen twigs, etc., taking worms and other small food. As the mouth is upwardly directed it can often be seen to twist around back downwards or to stand vertically in the water. This is a peaceful, sociable fish that has not yet been bred in captivity.

Chilodus punctatus

SPOTTED HEADSTANDER

Northern South America; 3 in.

A rather inconspicuously coloured fish with a very small mouth; it therefore feeds on fine live food and vegetable matter. This species has not become very widespread but has been bred a few times in large aquaria. It requires soft, slightly acid water at a temperature of 77–81°F.

Tube-Mouthed Pencilfish

Aponogeton crispus
Ceylon. A large plant requiring plenty of space. Not difficult, but prefers soft, slightly acid water and not too much light.

Striped Anostomus

**Spotted
Headstander**

flowering shoot

Black-Winged Hatchetfish

Marbled Hatchetfish

Common Hatchetfish

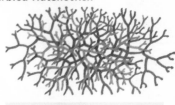

Riccia fluitans
Cosmopolitan. A hardy, floating plant.

FAMILY GASTERO-PELECIDAE

HATCHETFISHES

The hatchetfishes form a small characteristic family widely distributed in South America. The deep body shape is a result of the peculiar enlargement of the shoulder-girdle, especially the humerus, which is enormous. This causes the protrusion of the breast region which greatly resembles that of a bird and is likewise used as an anchorage for the large muscles of the pectoral fins. This is connected with a certain ability to beat these fins very rapidly and thus to leap out of the water and glide for a distance of 10–15 feet.

Hatchetfishes should be kept in soft, slightly acid water in a long tank with some vegetation; the water can be kept at 73–86°F. They should be given live food, particularly whiteworms, small crustaceans and midge larvae. Because of this leaping ability, aquaria containing hatchetfishes should always be covered.

Carnegiella marthae

BLACK-WINGED HATCHETFISH

Peru, Brazilian Amazon and Venezuela; 1½ in.

The smallest and least imported of the hatchetfishes mentioned here.

Carnegiella strigata

MARBLED HATCHETFISH

Amazon Basin and Guyana; 1¾ in.

In nature this species lives in small rain-forest streams completely overgrown by vegetation and with clear, brown, acid water. The marbled hatchetfish is the most frequently imported member of the group and is hardy and peaceful in the aquarium, although breeding has only been successful on a few occasions as the females do not normally spawn. There is usually no external difference between the sexes in hatchetfishes.

Gasteropelecus sternicla

COMMON HATCHETFISH

Guyana, Amazon Basin; 2½ in.

Found in large and small rivers, and even in quite small streams. Hardy, but rather sensitive to low temperatures. This species has not yet been bred in the aquarium.

Gyrinocheilus aymonieri

seen from below

One-Striped African Characin

Neolebias ansorgei

FAMILY
CITHARINIDAE

A small African family, closely related to the characins. Only a few species have become widespread as aquarium fishes.

Nannaethiops unitaeniatus

ONE-STRIPED AFRICAN CHARACIN

Equatorial Africa; 2½ in.

A very hardy species which spawns readily and is prolific. It is, however, rather shy and should preferably be kept in a separate large tank with plenty of plants and some sunshine.

A smaller species, *Nannaethiops tritaeniatus*, from the upper reaches of the Congo, is sometimes imported.

Neolebias ansorgei

West Central Africa; 1½ in.

A beautiful but shy bottom-living fish which only thrives in soft water; the temperature should be 75–84°F. Not difficult to breed, but it is sometimes difficult to rear the young, which require very fine food.

FAMILY
GYRINOCHEILIDAE

One genus with three species.

Gyrinocheilus aymonieri

Thailand; 10 in.

This fish is specialized for rasping algae from leaves, using the large downward directed mouth which forms a sucking organ. There is a special opening through which the water passes into the gill-chamber so that the fish does not need to break off feeding in order to allow water to pass through the gills. Since it was first imported in 1958 this fish has become very popular as a cleaner in the aquarium, particularly for removing soft algae and it is unsurpassed for this job. Strangely enough, this undemanding fish has not yet been bred in captivity. Its only disadvantage is that as it matures it may become aggressive towards other species. In addition it is almost impossible to catch as it is very quick and will hide deep in the vegetation as soon as it sees a net. So one has to empty the tank to catch it.

Citharinidae

Gyrinocheilidae

Gasteropelecidae

48

FAMILY CYPRINIDAE

A widespread family, rich in species, which are found in fresh waters from the arctic regions to the tropics. About 150 species are known, of which only a few can be considered as aquarium fishes. The carps have no adipose fin, but usually have one or two barbels.

Barbus

THE TRUE BARBS

A genus with a large number of species,

distributed in the subtropics and tropics of the Old World. In recent literature the generic name *Puntius* has often been used instead of *Barbus*. When correctly used, this name refers only to the tropical barbs which lack barbels, whereas the tropical species with two barbels should be placed in the genus *Capoeta*, tropical species with four barbels should be called *Barbodes*, and the name *Barbus* is limited to the European barbs. However, it is most practical to regard these three names as subgenera so that the correct generic name is still *Barbus*. The tropical barbs are generally beautiful and hardy aquarium fishes that prefer a spacious tank with a soft, dark bottom and some densely planted areas.

Barbus nigrofasciatus

BLACK RUBY BARB

Southern Ceylon; 2 in.

Occurs in the calm, slow-flowing parts of mountain streams with dense vegetation. This is one of the most beautiful

barbs and is easy to breed at a temperature of 77–82°F and is very prolific. It likes plenty of sunshine.

Barbus tetrazona tetrazona

SUMATRA BARB

Sumatra and Borneo; 2½ in.

Often known as the tiger barb, this is a magnificent, hardy, schooling fish which is only suitable for large tanks with fresh, clear water. Sometimes difficult to breed, it spawns most readily when kept in a school but all the adults should be removed after spawning, as they will devour both eggs and young. There are no conspicuous sex differences but the female is normally stouter than the male.

Barbus tetrazona partipentazona

Thailand; 2½ in.

Care and breeding as for the Sumatra barb. Both of these subspecies of *B. tetrazona* are very prolific and a female may lay 600–1000 eggs at one spawning. These hatch in 24–30 hours and the fry should be fed on very fine food.

Barbus pentazona

FIVE-BANDED BARB

Malay Peninsula, Borneo; 2 in.

A more difficult fish to keep and breed than the previous two forms. It should be kept in soft, slightly acid water in a large densely planted tank, at a temperature of 81–86°F.

> **Cryptocoryne petti**
> *Ceylon. The species of* Cryptocoryne *from Ceylon are more easily kept as submerged water plants than those from South-east Asia.*

49

Black Ruby Barb ♂ ♀

Sumatra Barb

B. t. partipentazona

Five-Banded Barb

Barbus gelius

GOLDEN DWARF BARB

Bengal and central India; 1½ in.

A peaceful, small barb which is unfortunately seldom seen in aquaria. It prefers a fairly low temperature, 68–71°F and in winter 61–64°F is sufficient.

Golden Dwarf Barb

♂

B. arulius

Barbus arulius

South eastern India; 4½ in.

One of the larger barbs which, because of its size, is not common in aquaria. In the adult male the individual fin rays are produced, whereas in the female the edge of the dorsal fin remains entire.

This species is easy to keep and breed at a temperature of 75–77°F, but is not very prolific. The eggs hatch in 24 hours and the fry hang for a week until they have absorbed the egg yolk and then begin to swim freely. The young fishes assume the colours of the parents when they are six months old. *Barbus filamentosus* is a very similar, but darker species.

Barbus oligolepis

ISLAND BARB OR CHECKERBOARD

Sumatra; 2 in.

A peaceful and hardy bottom-living fish which, like most other barbs, spawns very readily. For breeding it is best kept in a tank densely planted with fine-leaved plants and with a bottom of small stones. This allows the eggs to sink down among the pebbles and thus escape the pursuit of the parents. The water should be soft and slightly acid (4–8 DH, pH about 7) and kept at a fairly high temperature. The parents should be removed immediately after spawning and the breeding tank should be darkened for the first few days.

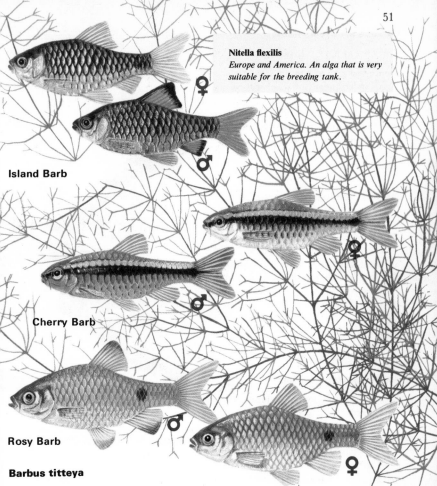

Nitella flexilis
Europe and America. An alga that is very suitable for the breeding tank.

Island Barb

♀

♂

Cherry Barb

♀

♂

Rosy Barb

♂

♀

Barbus titteya

CHERRY BARB

Ceylon; 2 in.

A rather shy barb which thrives best in a richly planted tank where it will often remain hidden. Temperature 75–77°F. Like many other barbs it likes a vegetarian diet, especially soft algae, but should be given whiteworms during the spawning period. It breeds in the same way as the other barbs, and a successful spawning will produce 200–250 offspring. The two sexes are similar in colour, except at spawning time when the male becomes brilliant red.

Barbus conchonius

ROSY BARB

Northern India, Bengal, Assam; in nature 5½ in., in the aquarium much smaller.

One of the classic aquarium fishes, previously very widespread and popular, but now less common. Normally the rosy barb is rather dull in colour, but at spawning time the male becomes a brilliant red. This is an extremely hardy fish which spawns readily.

Barbus semifasciolatus

GREEN BARB OR CHINA BARB

South-east China; 3 in.

An undemanding fish which will tolerate low temperatures, but should be bred at 71–75°F in clear fresh water, in a large well-planted tank kept in a sunny position. The female is duller in colour than the male and distinctly plump at spawning time.

Green Barb

Barbus 'schuberti'

GOLDEN BARB

This is now a popular and widespread barb in aquaria as it is beautiful and very robust, although there is some mystery as to its origin. It was first noticed in aquarium stocks in North America and it is probably a mutation from *Barbus semifasciolatus*. The name *'schuberti'* is not scientifically valid.

Barbus schwanenfeldi

SCHWANENFELD'S BARB

Sumatra, Borneo, Malay Peninsula, Thailand; 13 in.

Juveniles of this elegant fish are often seen in the aquarium trade and are usually bought by aquarists who are unaware how large they become. This is a species which should only be acquired after one has considered what to do with it when it grows too big for the tank. It is undemanding, peaceful and omnivorous. The water temperature should be 71–77°F.

Caecobarbus geertsi

BLIND BARB

Caves in the Congo Basin, near Thysville; 3 in.

Like the blind cave-fish *(Anoptichthys)* this species is blind and without pigment. Although it is hardy, it has never been bred in the aquarium. This, together with the fact that it is totally protected in its native country, means that it is very rarely seen on the market. Unfortunately the protection laws are sometimes broken and it is included in import batches.

Barbus stoliczkanus

STOLICZKA'S BARB

Burma; 2½ in.

An attractive, undemanding barb which breeds quite readily at 75–79°F. The female is more heavily built than the male and is paler in colour and usually lacks the dark tip of the dorsal fin.

Cryptocoryne willisii
Ceylon.

Golden Barb

Schwanenfeld's Barb

Stoliczka's Barb

Blind Barb

GOLDFISH

VEILTAILS

Carassius auratus

GOLDFISH

This is the domesticated form of the Asiatic and east European form of *Carassius auratus*, from which the Chinese developed golden forms at least a thousand years ago. By subsequent selection and breeding they, the Koreans and the Japanese produced several other domesticated forms with greatly produced fins, a shortened, often deformed body, and sometimes, enlarged eyes. The goldfish is a cold-water fish which also becomes rather large; so it has not become popular as an aquarium fish and indeed it is not suitable as such. Goldfish are, however, hardy in garden pools, where they can be left during winter provided the water does not freeze solid.

The various veiltail forms, whose bizarre appearance has made them popular, are often delicate and should be kept in large aquaria. They cannot tolerate temperatures below 59°F and are best bred in early spring in clear, neutral water at 68–73°F. They should not be kept together with other species, which may damage their unnaturally long, delicate fins.

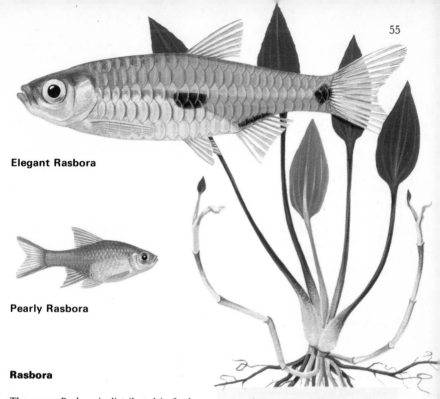

Elegant Rasbora

Pearly Rasbora

Cryptocoryne nevillii
Ceylon. A slow-growing plant.

Rasbora

The genus *Rasbora* is distributed in fresh waters from East Africa to the Philippines and consists mainly of small, peaceful, colourful species which are therefore among the most popular aquarium fishes. They are primarily schooling fishes that frequent the open areas in still or flowing waters, but some of the more colourful species occur in small pools filled with vegetation.

Rasbora lateristriata

ELEGANT RASBORA

Malay Peninsula; 5 in.

One of the larger and therefore not very popular species of *Rasbora*. The female is stouter and paler than the male. This is a prolific species which breeds readily in soft, neutral to slightly acid water, which should be well matured.

Rasbora vaterifloris

PEARLY RASBORA

Ceylon; 1½ in.

With its delicate, reddish pearly sheen, this is one of the most beautiful of the *Rasbora* species. Although frequently imported, healthy specimens are rarely seen because it is very difficult to keep. The closely related species *Rasbora nigromarginata* can be distinguished from *R. vaterifloris* by its more brilliant red coloration. When imported it is often sold under the name *R. vaterifloris*. Both species are difficult to breed and require soft, slightly acid water (1·5–2·5 DH, pH 6·3–6·7). In both species the males have larger fins than the females.

Rasbora heteromorpha

HARLEQUIN FISH OR RASBORA

Malay Peninsula, Thailand, Eastern Sumatra; 1¾ in.

The harlequin fish is one of the most beautiful fishes and is not at all exacting in its requirements, so it is not surprising that it is also one of the most popular of aquarium fishes. For many years it was an expensive rarity, but it is now bred in large numbers in South-east Asia and can be bought in any pet shop. In addition, it is no longer the problem fish it was in the early years and is now bred by many private aquarists. It spawns in soft, slightly acid water at 75–82°F. The eggs are deposited on the underside of the leaves of aquarium plants and they hatch in 24–28 hours.

Rasbora hengeli

Sumatra; 1¼ in.

This fish is very similar to the harlequin fish, but is slimmer and duller in colour, and the wedge in the rear half of the body is narrowed.

Rasbora maculata

SPOTTED RASBORA

Malay Peninsula, Sumatra; 1 in.

When in good condition this species is brilliantly red. It breeds in soft, acid water, preferably with a dark bottom such as peat.

Rasbora urophthalma

Sumatra, in small, still pools with soft, acid water; 1 in.

A peaceful, hardy fish. It has no place in an ordinary community tank, but a small tank with *R. urophthalma, R. maculata* and *Epiplatys annulatus* can be an exceptionally beautiful sight.

This fish mates readily and spawning, which often lasts for more than three or four days, usually takes place in a small clump of fine-leaved plants. The young should be fed with infusorians and growth is very rapid.

The female has no black marking on the dorsal fin.

Rasbora trilineata

SCISSORS-TAIL RASBORA

Malay Peninsula and Indonesia; 6 in.

A fairly large, elegant fish which is easy to keep. The popular name refers to the characteristic cutting movements made by the caudal fin.

Rasbora dorsiocellata

EYE-SPOT RASBORA

Malay Peninsula, Sumatra; 2½ in.

A hardy and very prolific Rasbora which is easy to breed.

Rasbora borapetensis

Thailand; 2 in.

This species is imported regularly but is not known to have bred in the aquarium.

Rasbora pauciperforata

RED-STRIPED RASBORA

Sumatra; 3 in.

Breeding takes place in soft, slightly acid water (pH 5·3–5·7) and is by no means easy.

Ceratopteris thalictroides
WATER SPRITE
Cosmopolitan. A fast-growing floating and marsh plant, requiring plenty of light and nutrient.

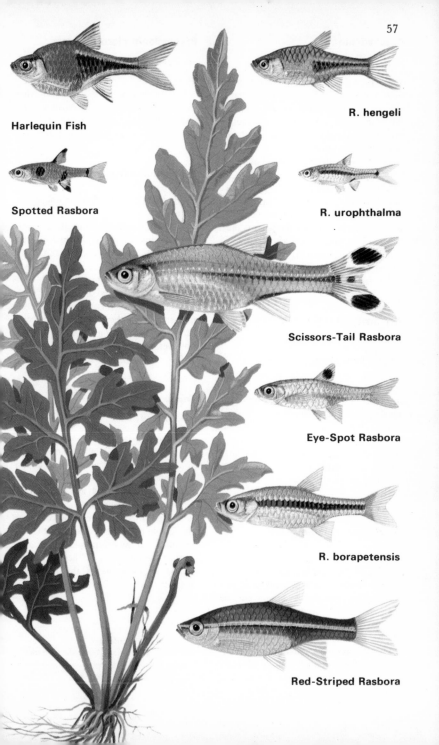

Harlequin Fish

R. hengeli

Spotted Rasbora

R. urophthalma

Scissors-Tail Rasbora

Eye-Spot Rasbora

R. borapetensis

Red-Striped Rasbora

Brachydanio

This genus of small barb-like fishes from southern Asia has become very popular with aquarists. It contains several hardy species which are ideal for the beginner. All of them can be kept in the community tank, which should be spacious and should have an open area for swimming. The water should preferably be hard and new, and maintained at a temperature of 71–73°F. If the water is suitable and the tank is kept in a sunny position, the pairs will spawn readily. The eggs are deposited amongst the plants, and the parents must be removed immediately after mating or they will eat their own eggs. The fry can be reared on very fine live food and pulverized dried food.

Brachydanio rerio

ZEBRA DANIO OR ZEBRA FISH

Eastern India; 1¾ in.

Except for some of the livebearing toothcarps, this is very much *the* beginner's fish. Not that it should be overlooked by the experienced aquarist, for a small school of well-fed zebra danios will embellish any aquarium. The female is larger and stouter than the male, and is sometimes a little duller in colour. The breeding temperature should not exceed 75°F.

Brachydanio albolineatus

PEARL DANIO

South-east Asia and Sumatra; 2 in.

This species is just as hardy and easy to keep as the zebra danio, but the temperature for breeding should be 79–82°F. With its changeable, iridescent coloration, this is an unusually beautiful fish in a well-lit, spacious aquarium. There are several different colour forms, of which the golden and the bluish are particularly fine.

Brachydanio nigrofasciatus

SPOTTED DANIO

Burma; 1½ in.

Smaller and rather more delicate than the other species of *Brachydanio*, the spotted danio is also more peaceful and it is not so much a schooling fish as its relatives.

Brachydanio frankei

South Asia (exact distribution unknown); 1¾ in.

A recently imported but already very popular, undemanding *Brachydanio* species. Information on the origin of the first specimens appears to be rather confused. As it has not been imported since, but has been exclusively bred in aquaria, there have been suggestions that it is merely a mutation of another *Brachydanio* species. More detailed anatomical investigations, however, appear to show that *B. frankei* is, in fact, a species in its own right.

Danio malabaricus

GIANT DANIO

West coast of India, Ceylon; 5 in.

The genus *Danio* is only separated from *Brachydanio* by the presence of an unbroken lateral line. *D. malabaricus* has not become so widespread in the aquarium world, as it grows rather long and needs a large, spacious aquarium. The colours of the female are more muted than those of the male and the central blue stripe has a distinct upward turn at the base of the caudal fin, whereas in the male it is straight.

Ludwigia alternifolia
North America. A hardy, fast-growing marsh plant which prefers a relatively low temperature.

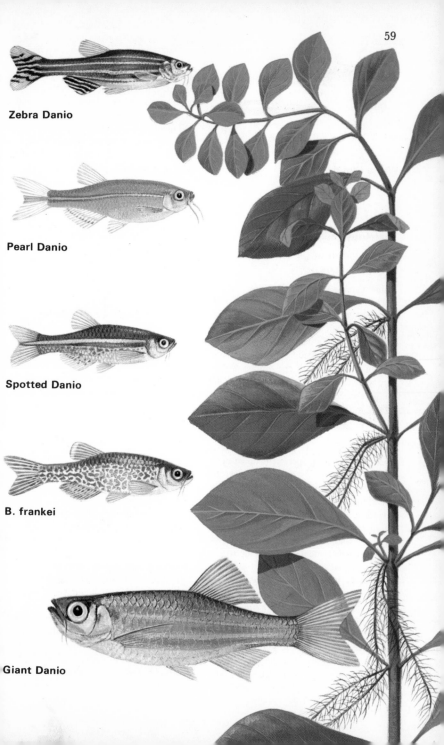

59

Zebra Danio

Pearl Danio

Spotted Danio

B. frankei

Giant Danio

White Cloud

Tanichthys albonubes

WHITE CLOUD MOUNTAIN MINNOW
OR WHITE CLOUD

China, Canton; 1½ in.

This fish is best kept at 64–68°F and does not thrive at temperatures above 71°F, although it will endure higher temperatures. In a densely planted aquarium it will spawn readily, and the parents do not usually molest the young, which can be reared in the breeding tank. The young are even more beautiful than the adults, as the iridescent green lateral band is very prominent.

The White Cloud Mountain minnow was described in 1932 by the Chinese zoologist Lin, from specimens taken near Canton. In 1939 the same zoologist wrote a description of another fish, *Aphyocypris pooni*, the Venus fish, which he had found on some islands off Hong Kong. This manuscript was sent to an American zoologist who, as he thought it had already been published, mentioned it in an article and at the same time gave a description of what he believed was *A. pooni*. Since Lin's manuscript had not, however, been published, the American's description had priority (see page 15). Complications arose when it was found that the fish that the American took to be the Venus fish was really only a local race of *Tanichthys albonubes* from Hong Kong. This was first discovered quite recently and the genuine Venus fish, which has had no name during all these years was then renamed *Hemigrammocypris lini*. The Venus fish mentioned in the literature is only a race of the White Cloud, and the name *A. pooni* is a synonym of *T. albonubes*. The genuine Venus fish, *H. lini*, which looks quite different from the White Cloud, has only been imported a few times into the U.S. and probably never into Europe.

Balantiocheilus melanopterus

Thailand, Borneo, Sumatra; 14 in.

An elegant, hardy fish which is rather large for most aquarists. It should be kept at 73–79°F, but it has not yet been bred.

Epalzeorhynchus kallopterus

Sumatra, Borneo; 3 in.

A handsome but rather inactive fish, which spends most of its time on the bottom, supported by the pectoral fins. It is a great consumer of algae and it also eradicates planarians. It has not yet been bred in the aquarium.

Labeo bicolor

RED-TAILED SHARK

Thailand; 5 in.

Although it has only recently been imported and has only been bred a few times in captivity, this fish has become very widespread and popular. It can be extremely aggressive, especially towards members of its own species. It prefers soft water and subdued lighting. In nature it feeds to a large extent on algae, which it grazes from rocks, roots and the like, and its diet in the aquarium should therefore include some vegetable matter. The common name is misleading, as this fish bears absolutely no relationship to the true sharks.

61

Balantiocheilus melanopterus

Epalzeorhynchus kallopterus

Red-Tailed Shark

62

Coolie Loach

A. k. sumatranus

A. myersi

A. semicinctus

FAMILY COBITIDAE

LOACHES

A family of rather small, mainly bottom-living fishes in which the mode of existence is reflected in their appearance: the mouth is directed downwards and is furnished with barbels. Characteristic of the family is a spine situated obliquely below the eye. This spine can be raised and is undoubtedly an effective weapon against predatory fishes.

Acanthophthalmus kuhlii

COOLIE LOACH

Indonesia; 3 in.

Various species of *Acanthophthalmus*, all called coolie loaches, are regularly seen on the market. They are best kept in a separate dark, sparsely planted tank, without other fishes to disturb them, and they will then give much pleasure to the aquarist. They are not difficult as regards type of water, temperature or food, and they will search eagerly along the bottom for anything edible. On the other hand, it is extremely difficult to get the *Acanthophthalmus* species to breed and they have not yet been bred in captivity under controlled conditions.

Acanthophthalmus kuhlii occurs in two races, *A. k. kuhlii* and *A. k. sumatranus*.

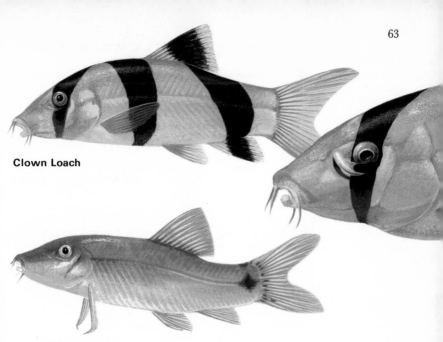

Clown Loach

B. modesta

Other forms imported are the closely related *Acanthophthalmus myersi* from Thailand (3 in.), and the more aberrant *Acanthophthalmus semicinctus* from Indonesia (3 in.).

Botia macracanthus

CLOWN LOACH

Sumatra, Borneo; 12 in., much smaller in aquaria.

The most popular of the loach group because of its brilliant colours and beautiful pattern. Newly-imported fish are often extremely delicate and particularly susceptible to white spot *(Ichthyophthirius)*, which is difficult to cure. If they avoid disease, however, they are hardy and excellent aquarium fish which, in contrast to many other loaches, are school forms. Indeed, they sometimes school with other fishes having the same coloration. This species has never been bred in captivity, and there are some theories that in nature it perhaps migrates into other types of water. As with the other loaches, care must be taken when catching them that the long preorbital spines, which are raised in times of danger, do not become entangled in the net, thus injuring the fish. A few other species of the genus *Botia* are imported from time to time, e.g. *B. modesta* from South-east Asia (4 in.). They resemble *B. macracanthus* in body form, behaviour and aquarium requirements, but are not so handsome.

CATFISHES

The catfishes (sub-order *Siluroidea*) are distributed in fresh waters in all parts of the world, with the exception of the very cold regions, and there are also a few representatives in sea water. They are characterized by the barbels at the sides of the upper jaw. Several also have barbels on the lower jaw. The sub-order contains approximately 2000 species, of which many are imported as aquarium fishes from time to time, but only a few can be said to be well-established in the aquarium, and very few are regularly bred. New and rare species are constantly appearing on the market.

FAMILY SILURIDAE

Distributed in Europe and Asia. The wels or European catfish, *Silurus glanis*, which can reach a length of more than 10 feet, belongs to this family.

Kryptopterus bicirrhis

GLASS CATFISH

South-east Asia, Indonesia; 3½ in.

This strange fish, as transparent as glass, differs from most other catfishes in that it lives in schools in the middle or upper water layers. It is very easy to keep as it has no special requirements as regards the type of water, temperature or food, although it does prefer live food and is best kept in a large tank with plants, at a temperature of 68–77°F. It is peaceful both towards its fellows and other species. It has not yet been bred. There are no external sexual differences.

FAMILY MOCHOKIDAE

A purely African family of scaleless catfishes.

Synodontis nigriventris

UPSIDE-DOWN CATFISH

Central Congo; 2½ in.

A widely distributed and very popular catfish, which is hardy and peaceful towards members of its own species. It has only been bred once. The upside-down catfish normally rests and swims belly-up and thus grazes the underside of leaves and roots taking live food and algae. As a result, the usual coloration found in nearly all fishes is reversed; normally a fish is darkest on its back and lightest on its belly. When the light falls on it from above it looks uniform in colour and thus loses its characteristic rounded shape so that it blends more easily with its surroundings. That this is the purpose of this countershading, which not only occurs in fishes, but also in many other animals, is shown by the opposite condition, i.e. a dark belly and a light back, which occurs in the few fishes, like the upside-down catfish, which swim upside down.

The very attractive *Synodontis angelicus* from West and Central Africa is rarely imported. The sharply contrasting colouring fades with age.

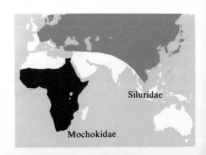

Siluridae

Mochokidae

Glass Catfish

Upside-Down Catfish

S. angelicus

young fish

Cryptocoryne griffithii
South-east Asia. Often called C. cordata, *a closely related species which is probably never imported.*

FAMILY CALLICHTHYIDAE

MAILED OR ARMOURED CATFISHES

Most of the catfishes that are kept in aquaria belong to this family, which is distributed in tropical South America, and the small members of the genus *Corydoras* are especially popular. These catfishes have a bony armour on the head, flanks and sometimes also down the back, and the pectoral fins have very powerful spines. In nature, they live mainly in small, slow-flowing, often stagnant watercourses where, if the oxygen content of the water is poor, they can survive by using the hindgut for respiration. Air is taken in through the mouth and passed along the intestine, and the oxygen in it is extracted by the hindgut which is richly supplied with blood vessels. Like several other catfishes, they can wander on land in a sufficiently damp atmosphere. The mailed catfishes are hardy and interesting and carry out an important function by eating food remains on the bottom that would otherwise not be noticed, but they may soil the water by their bottom-digging activities. They are not particular about the type of water and can even live in badly polluted water. However, the water should preferably be neutral or slightly alkaline. They are virtually omnivorous and a few individuals in a community tank need no

special feeding, as they take whatever falls to the bottom of the food given to the other fishes. On the other hand, all the species are difficult to breed and many are so difficult that breeding attempts have never been successful. The females are normally larger and more plump than the males and often have a rounded dorsal fin in contrast to the pointed dorsal fin of the male. Breeding seems to be more likely in an aquarium with a soft, dark bottom and with several caves and roots where the fishes can hide and deposit their eggs. After mating, the female swims to a previously cleaned stone or root and lays the eggs there. The parents should be removed immediately, as they may destroy the eggs. The eggs hatch after five to eight days. It may be an advantage to have several males to one female. As the various *Corydoras* species are almost identical as regards their biology and aquarium requirements, only their names and distribution are given below.

Corydoras aeneus
BRONZE CORYDORAS
Venezuela and Trinidad, southwards to the La Plata system; 2 in.

Corydoras hastatus
DWARF CORYDORAS
Amazon Basin; 1¼ in.

Corydoras arcuatus
ARCHED CORYDORAS
Amazon Basin; 2 in.
South-eastern Brazil and the La Plata area; 2½ in.
    This species is the most ready spawner in the group.

Corydoras julii
LEOPARD CORYDORAS
Lower Amazon; 2 in.

Corydoras paleatus
PEPPERED CORYDORAS OR
PALEATUS CATFISH

Corydoras melanistius
BLACK-SPOTTED CORYDORAS OR
GUYANA CATFISH
Northern South America; 2 in.

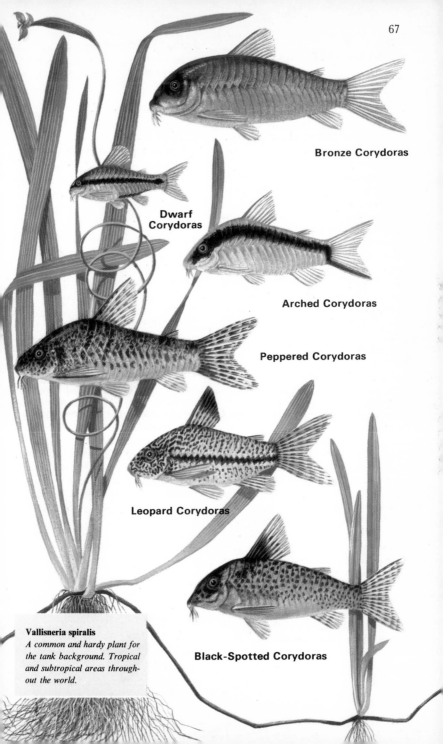

Bronze Corydoras

Dwarf Corydoras

Arched Corydoras

Peppered Corydoras

Leopard Corydoras

Black-Spotted Corydoras

Vallisneria spiralis
A common and hardy plant for the tank background. Tropical and subtropical areas throughout the world.

FAMILY LORICARIIDAE

SUCKERMOUTH CATFISHES

A family of catfishes confined to South America and adapted to life in fast-flowing waters. In such streams the fishes must be able to avoid being swept away by the current and must be able to utilize the often poor food supply in such rapidly flowing water. The principal adaptation for this way of life can be seen in the shape and position of the mouth, for the Loricariidae have a sucking mouth with broad, lobed lips on the underside of the head. In their natural surroundings, they can be seen to move in small hops from place to place. It is primarily the whole shape of the body which prevents them being carried away by the current. Because of the hollow oral disc, the slightly arched back and concave belly, the water flowing past creates currents which press the fish down on to the bottom. The mouth is mainly used for taking food and in an area with such a poor food supply it is an advantage to have large lips, which are used to graze the thin layer of algae from roots and stones.

In the aquarium these fishes do not require running water, but they do need a vegetable diet, and even in tanks with an abundance of algae there is not usually enough. The diet should, therefore, be supplemented with boiled spinach. They are not particular about temperature (70–77°F) and type of water and some species have been bred in captivity. They have a complicated courtship and the eggs are deposited on a previously cleaned root or stone. The eggs hatch in nine to twelve days and both the eggs and the newly born young are guarded by the male. In at least one species of *Loricaria* the eggs are carried about on the female's lower lip.

Loricaria filamentosa

Northern South America; 8 in.

Otocinclus flexilis

La Plata; 2 in.

A small, peaceful species which can be warmly recommended as a consumer of algae in community tanks.

FAMILY MALAPTERURIDAE

Contains only the following species:

Malapterurus electricus

ELECTRIC CATFISH

Central Africa and the Nile valley; 4 in.

Because of its size and aggressive behaviour, the electric catfish is not really suitable for the private aquarium, although it is easy to keep. It is, however, quite often seen, because of the interest which always surrounds those fishes which have electric organs. The electric catfish can give a very unpleasant shock, and although it is not dangerous to humans it can paralyze smaller fishes in the same tank. Apparently the electric organ of this species is not used for orientation, as in the electric eel and many other electric fishes, but only as a weapon for attack and defence.

Malapteruridae

Loricariidae

Loricaria filamentosa

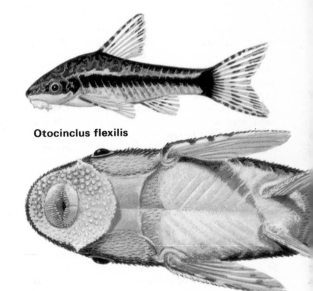

Otocinclus flexilis

the fish seen from below

Electric Catfish

FAMILY CYPRINODONTIDAE

KILLIFISHES OR EGGLAYING TOOTHCARPS

A family rich in species, distributed in all the tropical and subtropical areas of the world, with the exception of Australia. These are small to medium-sized, often beautifully coloured fishes which are characterized by the lack of barbels and by possessing teeth.

The egg-laying toothcarp family contains a large number of species, whose systematics are still not fully understood. Some of the most magnificently coloured aquarium fishes are to be found among them. However, many of the species should only be kept by the experienced aquarist and it must be emphasized that many of the species should be kept in special tanks because of their aggressive behaviour. Normally a single male is kept with several females, in quite a small heavily planted tank where there should be places to hide, since the male may otherwise chase the females to death.

Aphanius iberus

In puddles, ponds and ditches along the Mediterranean coast of Spain and northern Morocco; 2 in.

A very hardy species and easy to breed. It has not become very widespread in aquaria, and in nature it is in the process of being exterminated by the introduced *Gambusia affinis*.

Jordanella floridae

AMERICAN FLAGFISH

Florida, in coastal swamps and lagoons; 2½ in.

A very hardy species which thrives in all types of water, preferably at fairly low temperatures (65–75°F); it prefers plant food. It is easy to breed, the eggs being deposited on the bottom, sometimes in a hollow made by the male. This species is unique amongst the toothcarps in that the male guards the eggs. The female should be removed from the tank immediately after spawning.

Cynolebias nigripinnis

ARGENTINE PEARL FISH

Probably from the La Plata Basin; 2 in.

The exact origin of the aquarium strain is not known. It is quite easy to breed, the eggs are very hardy, and they sometimes lie for a long time, up to three years, without hatching (see p. 72).

Other species of the genus *Cynolebias* are imported, including *C. belotti* from the La Plata Basin (3 in.), and *C. whitei* from Brazil (♂ 3 in., ♀ 2 in.). The species of *Cynolebias* seem to prefer relatively low temperatures. The *Cynolebias* are called annual fishes because they live in areas in which the ponds dry up at certain times of the year. The adults die but the eggs survive in the bottom mud until the rainy season returns.

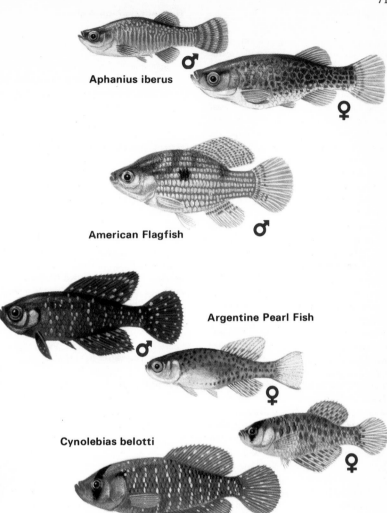

Aphanius iberus ♂ ♀

American Flagfish ♂

Argentine Pearl Fish

Cynolebias belotti ♂ ♀

Chriopeops goodei ♂

BLUE-FIN KILLY

Florida; 2 in.

Should be kept in a densely planted tank at 66–73°F. It spawns readily at 68–75°F but the parents are notorious egg-eaters, and must therefore be removed from the tank. The eggs hatch in 10–12 days and the young require very fine food.

Blue-Fin Kelly ♂

Nothobranchius

The genus *Nothobranchius* contains about twenty species distributed in small streams and water-holes in East and Central Africa.

The members of this genus are annuals, that is, they reach sexual maturity during a single rainy season. They then lay their eggs, the water dries up and the parents die. The eggs are able to withstand the period of drought and they hatch in the next rainy period when the water-hole is again filled. Such eggs do not normally hatch out unless they have been subjected to this period of drying-out, and some eggs in a brood may not even hatch until they have been dried out several times. This means that in nature they will not hatch after the first short shower, which may occur before the main rainy season starts. Even in aquaria the eggs must be allowed to dry and then be kept for some weeks or months in slightly damp sphagnum moss. The subsequent hatching is sometimes made easier if organic material that will rot is added to the water; the subsequent reduction in the amount of oxygen in the water may stimulate hatching. Many other killifishes are annuals, and the eggs of several species that are not normally annuals can tolerate similar desiccation.

The genus *Nothobranchius* includes some of the most beautiful of all aquarium fishes, and they are often to be found on the market. However, they are by no means easy to keep, and they should be purchased only by the experienced aquarist. They appear to thrive best in hard, neutral water. Only the males are brightly coloured. The females are so plain that they appear to be unrelated to their male counterparts.

The systematics of *Nothobranchius* species have been investigated very little, and the identification of imported specimens is often impossible because the locations from which they were taken are unknown; so some of the following names may be incorrect.

Nothobranchius rachovii

Coastal savannas in Mozambique; 2 in.

This species belongs to the so-called *N. taeniopygus* group which also includes *N. brieni* and *N. taeniopygus*. *N. rachovii* is the only member of the group that is regularly imported.

Nothobranchius guentheri

Nothobranchius palmquisti

Coastal lowlands of Tanzania; 2 in.

These two forms are very closely related and completely fertile hybrids can be produced between them. They should therefore probably be regarded as geographical races of one and the same species. They are separated by the colour of the caudal fin. The females are smaller than the males, are colourless and have smaller fins.

Nothobranchius brieni

Katanga; 2 in.

A rarely imported member of the *N. taeniopygus* group.

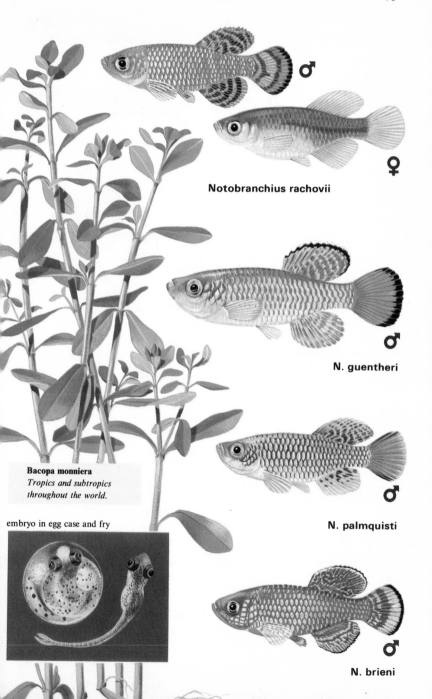

73

Notobranchius rachovii

♂

♀

N. guentheri

♂

N. palmquisti

♂

Bacopa monniera
*Tropics and subtropics
throughout the world.*

embryo in egg case and fry

N. brieni

♂

The genus *Epiplatys* contains about forty species, which are native to West and Central Africa. They are pike-like, predatory fish and are hardy in the aquarium. Although several species are imported from time to time, only a few have become widespread, as the majority are rather inactive and the coloration of some species is not particularly attractive. They do best in soft to medium-hard, neutral to slightly acid water at a temperature of 75–82°F.

Epiplatys dageti monroviae

FIREMOUTH EPIPLATYS

South-western Liberia; 2½ in.

Widely distributed amongst aquarists under the name *E. chaperi*. This species was imported into Germany in 1908, and some specimens were sent to the British Museum for determination. They were identified as *E. chaperi*, a species described in 1882 from specimens collected on the Ivory Coast. Only one pair survived the first few months in 1908, but this pair became the progenitors of the millions of 'E. chaperi', which have ever since been the most popular of the cyprinodontids. This shows that inbreeding is not necessarily harmful.

The confusion about the name began about 1960 when an *Epiplatys* was found in Ghana and the Ivory Coast which was identical to the original museum specimens of *E. chaperi*, but different from the aquarium strain of the same name. This aquarium strain had, therefore, to be renamed in 1964 as a result of the strict international rules of nomenclature. The true *E. chaperi* is imported, but has not become widespread, as it is aggressive and not very attractive.

E. dageti monroviae, distinguishable by the red throat of the male, is hardy, peaceful towards other species, and spawns

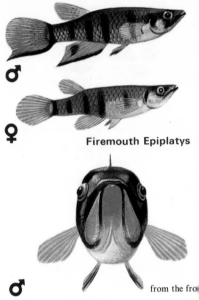

Firemouth Epiplatys

from the fro

Epiplatys sheljuzhkoi

readily among fine-leaf plants or nylon spawning mops.

Epiplatys sheljuzhkoi

South-western Ghana and the Ivory Coast; 3 in.

A beautiful and hardy but rather boisterous species which is suitable for a special, separate aquarium. It is closely related to the true *E. chaperi*.

Epiplatys bifasciatus

West Africa, watercourses in the savanna; 2 in.

A hardy, but not very widespread species which does well and breeds in hard water. The large eggs are laid near the surface of the water. The adult fish are shy; so the tank should be densely planted and should contain several of the same species.

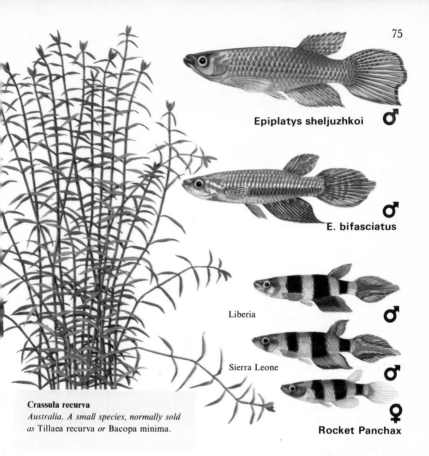

Epiplatys sheljuzhkoi ♂

E. bifasciatus ♂

Liberia ♂

Sierra Leone ♂

♀

Rocket Panchax

Crassula recurva
Australia. A small species, normally sold as Tillaea recurva *or* Bacopa minima.

Epiplatys annulatus

ROCKET PANCHAX

Guinea to Liberia; 1½ in.

The smallest and by far the most beautiful of the *Epiplatys* species. It is not often seen, as it appears to be rare in nature. It should be kept in a special tank. It is difficult to breed; apparently the embryo is often killed by bacteria which penetrate the egg membrane. For breeding, the water should be soft and acid (0 DH, pH 5·0–5·5).

The fry are very small and must be given the very finest live food, which they eat mainly from the surface. The populations from Sierra Leone and Liberia vary some-

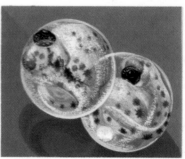

eggs about to hatch

what in coloration, particularly in the coloration of the fins, as shown in the illustration, but these two imported populations can be crossed.

Pachypanchax playfairi

Pachypanchax playfairi

Seychelles, Zanzibar and possibly East Africa; 4 in.

A robust, aggressive and extremely hardy species. The small eggs do not need to dry out before they start to develop. The colours of the female are duller than those of the male and the anal fin is rounded.

Pachypanchax homalonotus

Madagascar; 3½ in.

Is sometimes imported. It is a hardy species and easy to breed.

Aplocheilus

A genus with seven species which are native to Asia. These fishes are related to those in the genus *Epiplatys* from Africa, and they resemble them in many ways. The water should not be hard and the temperature is best kept in the range 68–77°F.

Aplocheilus lineatus

Southern India; 4 in.

A rather large and very hardy species which is often available on the market. The eggs are very large and they do not need to dry out before they hatch. The female has bolder transverse bands than the male and more rounded fins.

Aplocheilus dayi

CEYLON KILLIFISH

Ceylon; 3½ in.

Resembles the preceding species in general appearance and behaviour, but is possibly not closely related to it. It is, however, just as hardy and as easy to breed in the aquarium. The female has round fins which are almost colourless.

Aplocheilus panchax

PANCHAX

India, South-east Asia and Indonesia; 3 in.

A very hardy species, common in aquaria. The individual populations vary somewhat in nature and several sub-species have been recognized. The female is very similar to the male, but its body is less iridescent.

Aplocheilus blocki

GREEN PANCHAX OR MADRAS KILLIFISH

Southern India; 2 in.

A small peaceful species, which is rather more delicate than the others in this genus and is susceptible to fish tuberculosis when living in unclean water. In some populations the males lack the red spots on the sides.

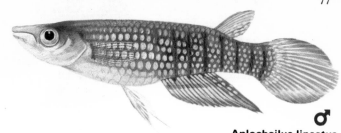

Aplocheilus lineatus ♂

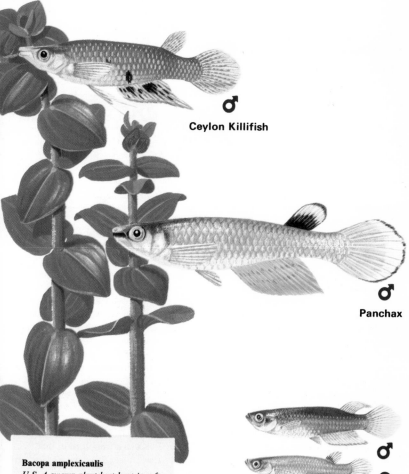

Ceylon Killifish ♂

Panchax ♂

Green Panchax ♂ ♀

Bacopa amplexicaulis
U.S. A swamp plant best kept in soft water at a low temperature.

Red Aphyosemion

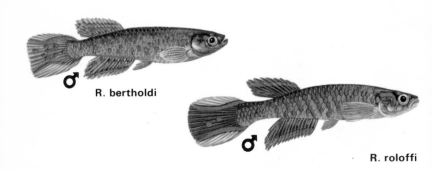

R. bertholdi

R. roloffi

Roloffia and Aphyosemion

Roloffia and *Aphyosemion* are so closely related that only specialists can distinguish between them; species of both genera were previously included under *Aphyosemion*. They are handsome fishes which, because of their aggressive behaviour, are not normally suitable for the community tank. However, they are much sought after by collectors, and as large numbers of eggs can be transported in a semi-dry state, there is a brisk international exchange. Although in nature the majority of the species occur in soft, acid water, in the aquarium it is easier to keep them free of fish tuberculosis in hard, alkaline water containing peat extract, or even better, with a bottom layer of sphagnum moss. Just before mating they should be transferred to soft, acid water.

Roloffia occidentalis occidentalis
RED APHYOSEMION
Sierra Leone; 3½ in.

This species is well known to aquarists under the name *Aphyosemion sjoestedti*. A very beautiful but rather large species, which is quite easy to keep and breed. The eggs require several weeks or months of drying-out before they will hatch. Several other species are imported, one of which is *Roloffia bertholdi* from woodland streams in eastern and possibly central Sierra Leone (2 in. in length). This is also easy to keep and breed, but the eggs do not appear to need the period of rest or drying-out. *Roloffia roloffia*, from southern Sierra Leone is also seen from time to time (2 in. long). Care and breeding as for the previous species.

The genus *Roloffia* is only found in West Africa.

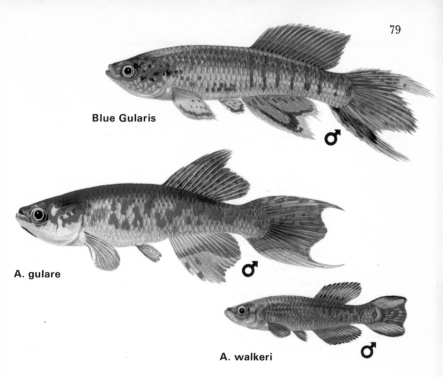

Blue Gularis

A. gulare

A. walkeri

Aphyosemion sjoestedti

BLUE GULARIS

Southern Nigeria, possibly western Cameroons, in swamps; 5 in.

In older literature, this species is called *A. coeruleum*, but this name is, by all accounts, invalid. It should not be confused with *Roloffia o. occidentalis*. A very large but interesting and quite hardy species. The eggs need a resting period before they will develop.

Aphyosemion gulare

Southern Nigeria; 3 in.

Care and breeding as for the preceding species. *Aphyosemion beauforti* and *A. fallax* are possibly synonyms of this species.

Aphyosemion walkeri

South-west Ghana and south-east Ivory Coast, in damp forests; 2½ in.

This species may be very delicate when kept in soft water. The eggs can develop without a resting period but they usually need one. *A. spurelli* is a synonym.

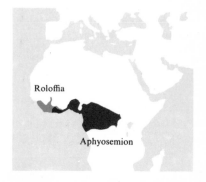

Roloffia

Aphyosemion

Aphyosemion gardneri

Nigeria and western Cameroons, in forest and savanna; 2 in.

There has been considerable confusion about the naming of this fish, which is a pity, as it has become one of the most widespread of the *Aphyosemion* species. Shortly after the first importation in 1957 it was identified as *A. calliurum*, but was later described under the name *A. nigerianum*, and eventually it was discovered that the correct name is *A. gardneri*. It is to be hoped that these name changes have now come to an end. This beautiful, but rather aggressive species is extraordinary in that the males occur in two different colour forms, one with, and the other without yellow bands on the fins. In nature both forms occur in the same populations. This is not therefore a question of different races but of what is termed polymorphism. One would expect that the colour phase that was best adapted, i.e. was less obvious to enemies, would eventually replace the other colour phase. This does not happen, however, and this is because the species, as such, benefits from the presence of two or more colour types amongst its individuals. It is believed that the mechanism is as follows: heterozygotes (crosses between the two colour phases) have more chance of survival than either of the pure types. Therefore, there will be positive selection for these heterozygous individuals, with the result that neither of the two phases will replace the other. This species should always be kept in a special tank, where the females have good opportunities for hiding from the aggresssive males.

Anubias lanceolata
West Africa. A slow-growing plant with submerged leaves.

Aphyosemion cinnamomeum

Mountain plateaus in western Cameroons; 2 in.

A beautiful, but very shy and rather inactive species which has not become very widespread. It is very susceptible to fish tuberculosis when kept in soft, acid water.

Aphyosemion calliurum

Southern Nigeria, in swamps; 2 in.

The genuine *A. calliurum* was imported into Germany as early as 1908 under the name *A. elegans*. Care and breeding as for the other members of the genus.

Aphyosemion filamentosum

PLUMED LYRETAIL

South-western Nigeria, in swamps; 2 in.

This species varies considerably within the limited area in which it occurs in nature. One of the varieties is sometimes called 'A. ruwenzori' by aquarists. As in the other species of this genus, the female is brownish and has transparent, rounded fins.

Aphyosemion christyi

Central Congo Basin; 2 in.

This species has not yet been investigated well enough in nature for its systematic status to be clear. A number of so-called biological species seem to be involved, i.e. forms that closely resemble each other in external appearance but cannot be interbred. The names *A. elegans, A. decorsei, A. castaneum* and *A. schoutedeni* refer to this species.

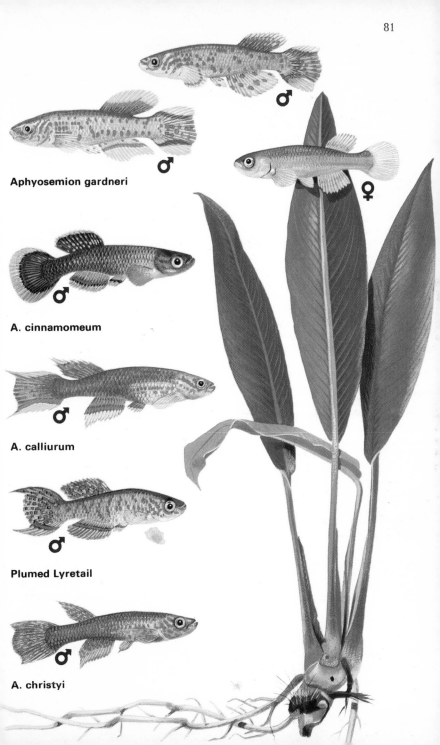

81

Aphyosemion gardneri ♂ ♂ ♀

A. cinnamomeum ♂

A. calliurum ♂

Plumed Lyretail ♂

A. christyi ♂

Aphyosemion bivittatum

In small- to medium-sized watercourses, in both forest and savanna from Togo to Spanish Guinea; 2 in.

One of the most popular species of *Aphyosemion* for the aquarium, and with good reason, as it is exceptionally colourful and small and peaceful enough to be kept in the community tank. In addition, it is hardy and easy to breed. This species has been studied extensively by Danish zoologists both in nature and in the aquarium and it has been found that it is composed of a number of populations in the different river systems – populations which in many cases have different chromosome numbers and cannot interbreed or will only do so with difficulty. There is therefore no doubt that these populations must be regarded as separate species, but as they are almost identical in external appearance only an expert can tell them apart. Because of the difficulty of identifying them, the whole complex (group) is still called *A. bivittatum.* However, future scientists will probably have to split this up into a number of species, each with its own name. *A. multicolor* is a synonym of *A. bivittatum.*

Aphyosemion australe

LYRETAIL

Gaboon and Brazzaville–Congo, in coastal swamps; 2 in.

A species that is assumed to be annual in nature, but the eggs can hatch without drying out. Easy to keep. It was one of the first *Aphyosemion* species to be imported and the only one from which a domesticated form has been produced, namely the golden lyretail, the so-called "*A. australe hjerreseni*". As it is a domesticated form and not a naturally occurring subspecies, it is technically incorrect to refer to it by a scientific name.

Aphyosemion bualanum

East Cameroons and Central African Republic, in savanna watercourses; 2 in.

In nature this species occurs in very different types of water from soft, slightly acid, to very hard and alkaline (0·5–20 DH). Thus, it follows that it is very easy to keep and breed in the aquarium. The young grow much more slowly than those of the other members of this genus.

Aphyosemion labarrei

Congo Basin; 2 in.
A beautiful and hardy species, imported into the U.S. in 1956 as blue panchax.

Aphyosemion exiguum

East Cameroons and northern Gaboon; $1\frac{1}{2}$ in.

A very recently imported and not very widespread species, which is attractive, hardy and easy to breed in all types of water. The young grow very slowly. It appears to be closely related to *A. bualanum.*

Sagittaria chilensis
Chile. Like the other Sagittaria *species this has submerged, floating and emerse leaves.*

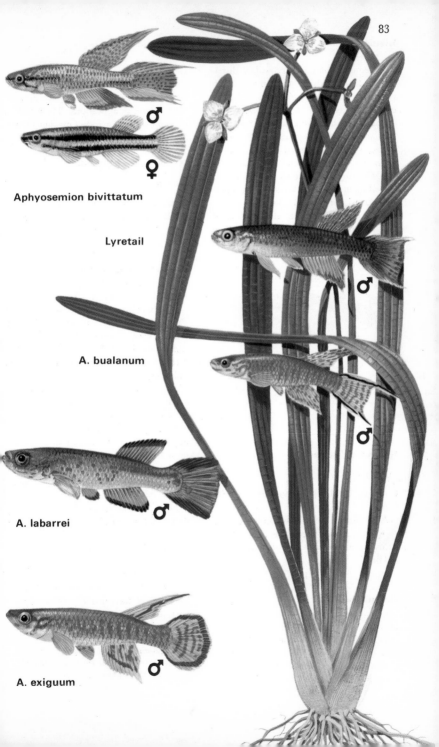

Aphyosemion bivittatum

♂

♀

Lyretail

A. bualanum

♂

♂

A. labarrei

♂

A. exiguum

♂

Rivulus

The genus *Rivulus* is very widely distributed, from Florida to central South America. The species are hardy and quite easy to breed; the best temperature is 71–82°F. Their colours are, however, less brilliant than those of most other killifishes, and so they are not so often seen in aquaria. Most of them are essentially surface-living fishes which in nature feed largely on mosquito larvae and insects that fall down onto, or fly just above the surface of the water; it also eats small fishes. Some species of *Rivulus* even like to lie on the floating leaves of aquarium plants.

Rivulus cylindraceus

CUBAN RIVULUS

Cuba, in fast-flowing mountain streams; 2 in.

A fish that can be warmly recommended. As in most *Rivulus* species the female has a clearly seen dark spot near the base of the tail fin.

Rivulus holmiae

Guyana and Surinam; 4 in.

This species is very closely related to *R. harti*, of which it is perhaps only a subspecies. The female has a clearly marked "rivulus spot" on the caudal fin.

Rivulus milesi

Colombia; 2 in.

A very hardy species which spawns readily and deserves to be popular because of its attractive appearance. The female is dark brown, again with a prominent spot at the base of the caudal fin.

Rivulus urophthalmus

GREEN RIVULUS

Amazon Basin and the Guianas; 2 in.

The female is duller than the male and has a dark spot at the base of the caudal fin.

Pterolebias longipinnis

Brazil, lower Amazon; 4 in.

An exceptionally beautiful species of *Pterolebias* which is unfortunately very seldom seen. It should be kept in soft, slightly acid water at 68–77°F (rather higher for breeding). One very rarely sees fully developed old males with long fins. The life of the adults is quite short, as they are annuals by nature. The aquarist should therefore only acquire young individuals and let them grow up in his tank. Specimens reared in the aquarium are often more brilliantly coloured than the bluish-grey imported fishes.

The female has shorter and less colourful fins than the male

In *Pterolebias* species the eggs need a drying-out period of 3–7 months.

Pterolebias peruensis

Upper Amazon; 3½ in.

A recently imported species which greatly resembles the previous one in appearance, behaviour and care. The female is smaller than the male and has shorter fins.

Sagittaria subulata f. natans
North America. Also known as S. natans.
Propagation by runners.

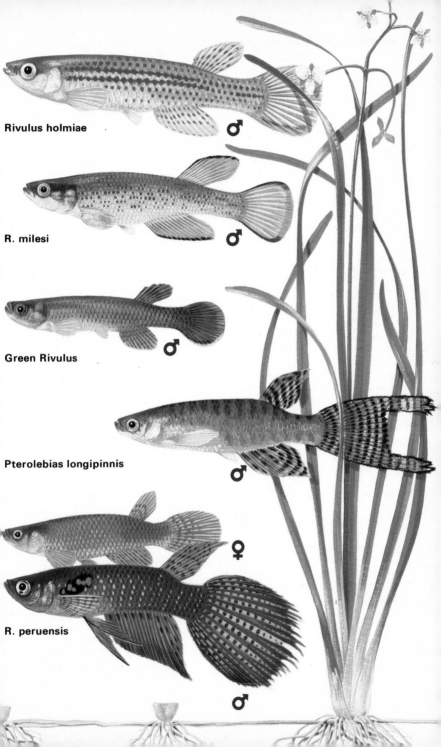

Rivulus holmiae ♂

R. milesi ♂

Green Rivulus ♂

Pterolebias longipinnis ♂

♀

R. peruensis

♂

Austrofundulus dolichopterus

Venezuela; $2\frac{1}{2}$ in.

A recently imported and rare small killifish, which was first described in 1963. It is not particularly colourful, but the male has peculiar, long dorsal and anal fins that are kept spread out, as shown in the illustration, even when the fish is swimming. In nature it lives in small shady pools with very soft, acid water. Although a peaceful fish it should undoubtedly be kept in a separate tank. The female is a more uniform brownish colour than the male and has shorter, paler fins.

Fundulus chrysotus

GOLDEN EAR KILLIFISH

South Carolina to Florida, westwards to Texas, in fresh and brackish water; 3 in.

The genus *Fundulus* is distributed in North and Central America, with numerous species. The members of this genus are not very colourful, and so have not become very widespread in Europe, and because they are natives, they are not highly valued in the U.S. Most species are easy to satisfy as far as temperature and type of water are concerned, but they require plenty of space and clumps of dense vegetation. Some are surface species, while others such as *F. chrysotus* are bottom-living fishes. The males may be aggressive towards the females.

Many of the species in this genus are found in brackish waters and therefore require the addition of salt to the water. Most of the species can also tolerate a very wide range of temperatures, from water close to freezing point to warm springs (99°F).

Oryzias latipes

JAPANESE MEDAKA

Japan, China, Korea; $1\frac{1}{2}$ in.

The small killifishes of the genus *Oryzias* from eastern Asia belong to a subfamily of their own. Various species are imported from time to time, and these are very similar to each other, so they are difficult to identify. They are all small, inconspicuously coloured schooling fishes that live in the open water. They can be kept in community tanks, as they are not aggressive towards other fishes. They are undemanding, both as regards temperature and type of water. The species of *Oryzias* will spawn readily, but the young are very difficult to rear. *O. latipes* is of particular interest because the female carries the fertilized eggs about in a cluster attached to her vent until they are brushed off on plants.

Oryzias minutillus

Thailand; $\male$ $\frac{1}{2}$ in., $\female$ $\frac{3}{4}$ in.

One of the smallest known fishes. The female only lays a few eggs (3–4) at a time and the young are almost impossible to rear.

Aplocheilichthys macrophthalmus

Rain-forest streams from south-eastern Dahomey to the River Niger in Nigeria; $1\frac{1}{2}$ in.

The small iridescent African species of *Aplocheilichthys* closely resemble the *Oryzias* species from eastern Asia, although they are not closely related.

They, too, are peaceful school fishes from the open water, but they are difficult to keep.

They seem to thrive best in quite hard, alkaline water, since it is easier to keep them free from disease in this way, but for breeding they require soft, slightly acid water. Breeding and rearing of the fry are difficult.

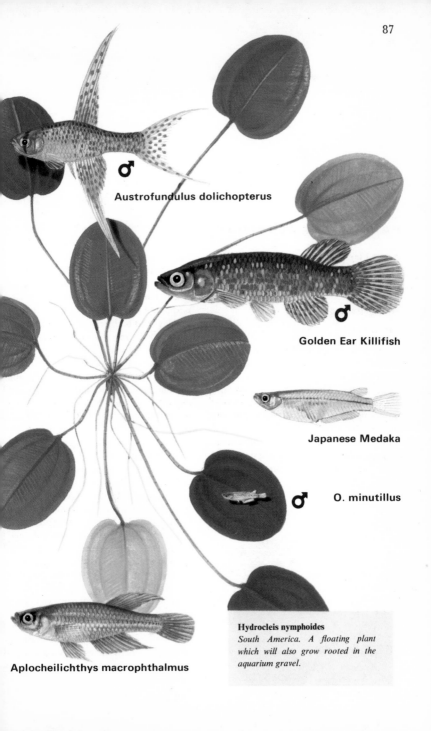

Austrofundulus dolichopterus ♂

Golden Ear Killifish ♂

Japanese Medaka

♂ **O. minutillus**

Aplocheilichthys macrophthalmus

Hydrocleis nymphoides
South America. A floating plant which will also grow rooted in the aquarium gravel.

Foureyes

FAMILY ANABLEPIDAE

A small family consisting of three species from central and northern South America.

Anableps anableps

FOUREYES

Fresh and brackish waters in north-eastern South America and Central America; 7 in.

This extraordinary fish always swims just at the surface of the water, with the water line running through the middle of the eye. The pupil of the eye is separated into two parts by a bridge and the retina is likewise divided. Fishes cannot normally focus clearly if their eyes are out of the

eye of anableps

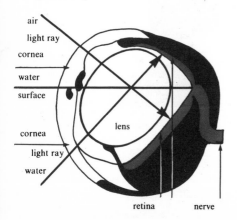

water, just as land animals cannot form a clear picture under water. Thanks to the shape of the lens the foureyes can focus clearly both above and below water. The purpose of this unique adaptation is that *Anableps* can both keep an eye on enemies under water and a look-out for insects which fall onto the surface of the water where they can be snapped up.

The female foureyes bears live young and the anal fin of the male is transformed into a gonopodium. Some males can only move this to the left, others only to the right, and this corresponds to the asymmetrical structure of the genital opening in the female. Thus, only males with a leftward-moving gonopodium can pair with a female having the genital opening on the right side, and vice versa. In a spacious aquarium with shallow water, good swimming space and clumps of vegetation this is a very hardy fish, though rather shy. It is peaceful towards other species, but may sometimes be aggressive towards members of its own species. Besides insects it eats *Daphnia* and dried food on the surface, but it can swim down to eat on the bottom only with difficulty. The young are few in number, only two to five, but they are very large and can take *Daphnia* and dried food immediately. Unfortunately this interesting fish is very seldom imported.

Pike Top Minnow

♂

FAMILY POECILIIDAE

LIVEBEARING TOOTH-CARPS OR GAMBUSINOS

A large family consisting mainly of small species from tropical and subtropical America. In all species the sperms are introduced into the female by the gonopodium of the male (the transformed anal fin), which can be moved forward during mating and pass into the genital opening of the female. In most species the eggs develop within the female so that the young have shed the egg membrane at birth or else they do so immediately afterwards. In many cases the female stores the sperm of the male for a long time so that several batches of eggs can be fertilized from a single mating, a phenomenon which one must take into consideration in breeding experiments. Many of the small species of the family are extremely hardy and very beautiful. These are classic aquarium fishes, to such an extent that the experienced aquarist is often scornful of them, which is a pity. Many species and genera are so closely related that they can hybridize, even in nature. Most species are hardy and will reproduce readily in a densely planted tank.

Salvinia auriculata
Tropical America. A floating plant which requires a high air humidity.

Belonesox belizanus

PIKE TOP MINNOW

Southern Mexico and northern Central America in fresh and brackish waters; ♂ ½ in., ♀ ¾ in.
A very interesting pike-like fish suitable for a separate, large, densely planted tank. It requires a very varied diet of live food, such as fishes (guppy size) or tadpoles. It is very easy to breed and a brood of a hundred is not uncommon. The water temperature should be 71–86°F.

Anablepidae

Poeciliidae

Least Killifish

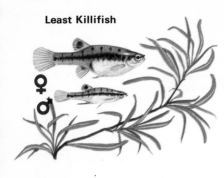

Heterandria formosa

LEAST KILLIFISH

South Carolina, Georgia and Florida, in fresh and brackish water; ♂ ¾ in., ♀ 1 in.

Because of its small size this attractive species can only be kept in a special tank on its own or with other very small fishes. It prefers relatively low temperatures, 68–75°F, but has no other special requirements. The female gives birth to only two young per day over a period of a week to ten days and these are not molested by the parents. An ideal fish for the beginner.

Gambusia affinis

GAMBUSIA

Southern U.S. and northern Mexico; ♂ 1 in., ♀ 2 in.

This species occurs in two races, *G. a. affinis*, which is uniform grey with a bluish sheen, and the more frequently seen *G. a. holbrooki*; some fish of either subspecies may show black markings. Both races are extremely hardy, spawn readily and thrive in any aquarium tank. Because they are so hardy they have been introduced into many subtropical and tropical areas (e.g. in large areas of southern Europe), to keep down the numbers of mosquito larvae in small pools.

Phalloceros caudomaculatus

CAUDO

Rio de Janeiro to Uruguay and Paraguay; ♂ 1 in., ♀ 2 in.

A very variable species, the black-spotted variety being the commonest form seen in aquaria. The caudo is hardy and can tolerate low temperatures (52–66°F), but does best at 68–75°F.

Girardinus metallicus

GIRARDINUS

Cuba; ♂ 1½ in., ♀ 2 in.

A hardy species which is seldom seen nowadays, as it is not so colourful as many other livebearing toothcarps. Temperature 71–77°F.

Limia melanogaster

BLUE LIMIA

Jamaica; ♂ 1 in., ♀ 2 in.

A beautiful species requiring high temperatures. In a recent systematic work the genera *Limia, Lebistes* and *Mollienisia* have been included under the generic name *Poecilia*, but for practical reasons the well-known aquarium names have been retained here.

The specific name 'melanogaster', meaning black-bellied, refers to the exceptionally large black pregnancy mark in the female. A similar, but smaller mark appears in the females of the other live-bearing toothcarps after the first mating.

Limia nigrofasciata

BLACK-BARRED LIMIA

Haiti; ♂ 1¾ in., ♀ 2 in.

Very beautiful, hardy and easy to spawn, this species is best kept at 71–77°F. Like so many other livebearers it requires plant matter (algae) as well as live food. With age the male develops a strongly arched back and a large dorsal fin.

91

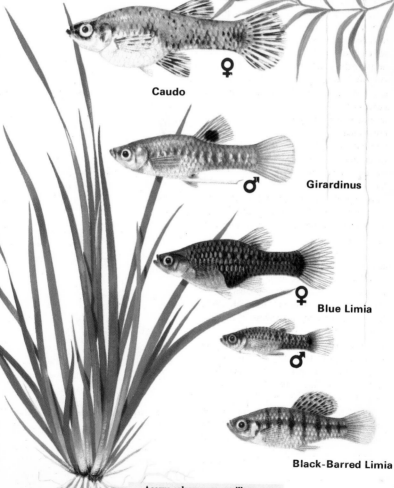

Gambusia affinis holbrooki

Najas graminea
South Europe, southern Asia, Africa. A hardy plant for the breeding tank. It grows without being rooted.

Caudo

Girardinus

Blue Limia

Black-Barred Limia

Acorus calamus var. pusillus
South Asia.

Lebistes reticulatus

GUPPY

Venezuela, Barbados, Trinidad, northern Brazil and Guyana; also introduced by man and now naturalized in so many places that the original distribution is unknown; ♂ 1 in., ♀ 2 in.

In nature the guppy appears to occur in all types of fresh waters and sometimes even in brackish water.

Since its first importation into Europe at the beginning of this century, the guppy has been one of the most popular aquarium fishes, the wild form mainly among less experienced aquarists because of its hardiness and readiness to mate, and the highly selected domesticated forms among experts. In the wild form the male is extremely variable and has thus proved to be one of the best experimental animals for the geneticist. This is because the various markings and patterns can be directly correlated with different genes (hereditary factors), and it has often been possible to determine the position of these genes on the chromosomes. The wild form is very hardy and thrives under the worst conditions, but it will only grow properly and breed satisfactorily if it is well fed and kept at a temperature that is not too low (71–75°F).

Since the genetics of this species has become so well known, it has been possible by systematic selection to produce a larger number of domesticated forms which are very different from the wild form in colour and in the shape of the fins. The aim of aquarium breeders is to produce strains that breed as pure as possible and at the same time are not so degenerate that there is a reduction in fertility or in their ability to carry the often large and heavy fins. New types are still being produced, others disappear, and the colour plate shows just a few of the numerous domesticated forms of the guppy.

Domesticated guppies are often much more delicate than the wild form. They require high temperature and are more susceptible to disease and there is also a great danger of degeneration due to inbreeding.

Because the guppy is so hardy and so exceptionally prolific, it has, like *Gambusia*, been introduced into many areas of the tropics and subtropics to keep down malaria mosquitoes. Thus the natural distribution pattern of the species has been obliterated.

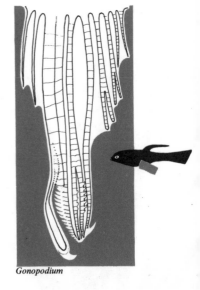

Gonopodium

Myriophyllum scabratum *(green stem)* and **M. rubrum** *(red stem)*

WATER MILFOIL

America. Prefers hard, slightly alkaline water.

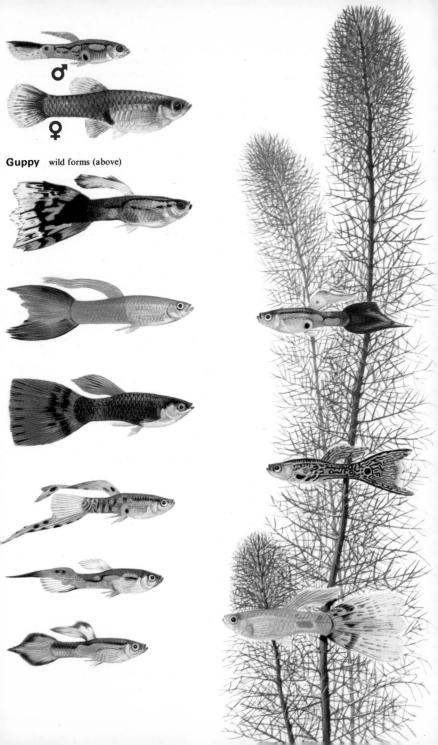

Guppy wild forms (above)

Mollienisia

The relatively large species of *Mollienisia*, now classified within the genus *Poecilia*, are among the most exclusive of the live-bearers. It is relatively easy to keep them alive, but it is very difficult to obtain large, healthy broods that develop as they should, and for some of the forms this is almost impossible, as they require so much space. The most beautiful specimens are fishes that have been bred in ponds in Florida.

Mollienisia species require plant food even more than the other livebearers if they are to develop satisfactorily. The following three species can be regarded as suitable for the aquarium.

Mollienisia velifera

Coastal waters of Yucatan; 6 in.

Mollienisia latipinna

South-eastern States of U.S. to Yucatan; 5 in.

Mollienisia sphenops

Texas to Colombia; ♂ 3 in., ♀ 5 in.

In nature these three species vary a great deal in coloration. Domesticated forms have been developed from all three and these have been further hybridized, so that it is impossible in many cases to give such forms a proper scientific name. The handsome enlarged dorsal fin is only seen in the males of *M. latipinna* and *M. velifera,* but these two species resemble each other so closely that one must be an expert to distinguish them.

The only constant difference is that *M. latipinna* has thirteen or fourteen dorsal fin rays, whereas *M. velifera* has eighteen. Presumably, the two species should only be regarded as races of a single species since, in nature, their own distribution areas border on each other, and they also hybridize very easily.

M. sphenops, with eight to eleven dorsal fin rays, never develops a large dorsal fin, but is just as beautiful as the others with its brilliant iridescent colours. This species is also very variable in nature.

Black varieties have been developed from all three species, and they are even more popular than the wild forms. One usually distinguishes between black velifera with a high, sail-like dorsal fin, black molly, with a long, low dorsal fin, which is possibly a domesticated form of *M. latipinna* and the liberty molly, a domesticated form of *M. sphenops*, with a small, rounded dorsal fin.

The lyretail molly, which has become very popular in recent years, was developed in South-east Asia where it is now bred in large numbers. It is not known from which species of *Mollienisia* it is derived. If they are to thrive, all the *Mollienisia* species require plenty of space, a vegetarian diet, warmth, and preferably the addition of a small amount of salt to the water. It is very important that different *Mollienisia* species should not be kept in the same tank, since they can all hybridize and the resultant offspring are seldom as beautiful as the parents.

Heteranthera dubia
U.S. to Cuba. Also known as H. graminea. *A hardy plant in alkaline water. Up to 6 ft. long.*

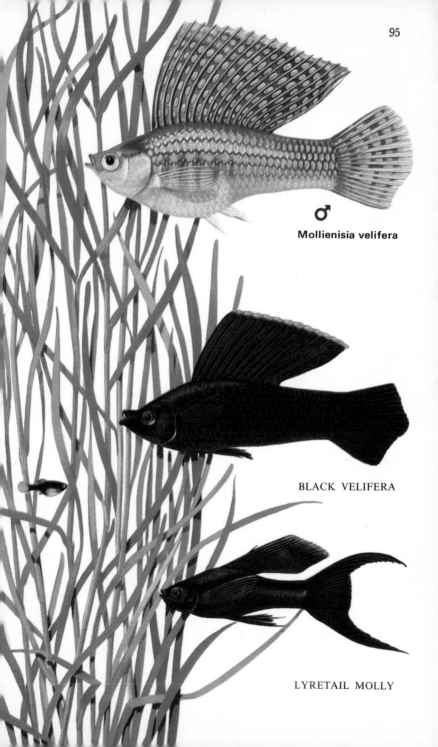

♂
Mollienisia velifera

BLACK VELIFERA

LYRETAIL MOLLY

Swordtail

Xiphophorus helleri

SWORDTAIL

East coast of southern Mexico, Guatemala; ♂ 3 in. plus sword, ♀ 5 in.

A very popular species. Although the coloration is quite constant in nature, the swordtail has proved to be capable of producing domesticated forms so that there are now swordtails with varying coloration and fin length. Some of these domesticated forms have been developed by crossing with varieties of *X. maculatus*. The swordtail is hardy and spawns readily, and it has no special requirements for temperature, food or type of water.

Xiphophorus maculatus

PLATY

Mexico to northern British Honduras, in the lowlands; ♂ 1½ in., ♀ 2 in.

A very popular aquarium fish in the U.S., where several different varieties such as the wagtail platy are kept.

Xiphophorus variatus

VARIATUS PLATY

East coast of Mexico; ♂ 2 in., ♀ 3 in.

This platy is very closely related to *X. maculatus*. In nature both species are variable, the most apparent difference between them being that *X. variatus* is slimmer than *X. maculatus* and usually has a dark longitudinal band along the sides of the body. There are several anatomical differences between *X. variatus* and *X. maculatus*.

From these fish which, in nature, are very variable, several domesticated forms have been developed in the aquarium. These have been made almost constant by controlled breeding which has gradually eliminated most of the genes which might induce reversion to the original 'wild' type of coloration. The wild types are rarely imported.

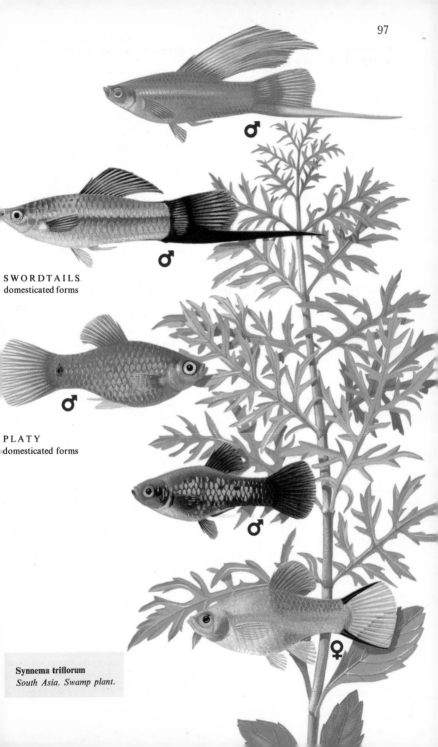

SWORDTAILS
domesticated forms

PLATY
domesticated forms

Synnema triflorum
South Asia. Swamp plant.

98

FAMILY HEMIRHAMPHIDAE

A small family of tropical and subtropical fishes, which are usually found in fresh and brackish waters.

Dermogenys pusillus

HALFBEAK

Distributed in South-east Asia, Indonesia and the Philippines in fresh and brackish waters, mostly in small streams and pools with dense vegetation; ♀ up to 3 in., ♂ smaller.

This is a surface-living fish which should be kept in a large tank with clumps of dense vegetation; otherwise it becomes nervous. It requires warmth but is hardy. Although it is livebearing it is difficult to breed; this may be because the parents are given an unbalanced diet. The period of gestation is three to eight weeks, the broods are usually quite small, but broods of up to thirty have been known. The young can be fed immediately after birth with small *Daphnia* and dried food given at the surface. They are not molested by the parents.

FAMILY CENTRARCHIDAE

SUNFISHES

A north American family closely related to the perches. The different species are seldom seen because cold-water aquaria are relatively uncommon.

Elassoma evergladei

PIGMY SUNFISH

North Carolina to Florida; 1 in.

This attractive little species is the most frequently seen pigmy sunfish and is extremely hardy. It is very tolerant to changes in temperature and can therefore be kept either in a heated tropical aquarium or in an unheated tank, as it can stand temperatures as low as 39°F. It appears to thrive best if it is kept at a low temperature in winter, and is seen to advantage in a small special tank. The broods are small (50–60) and the fry must be given the very finest live food. They are not attacked by the adults. The female does not have the beautiful dark colour of the male, but is red-brown with transparent fins. Two other species – *E. zonatum* and *E. okefenokee* – are sometimes collected. All three species are quite similar, but *E. okefenokee* is the more colourful.

Mesogonistius chaetodon

BLACK-BANDED SUNFISH OR CHAETODON

New Jersey to Florida; 2½ in.

This handsome native U.S. species thrives best in an unheated tank. The sexes are difficult to distinguish, but the female is normally paler than the male. Should be kept in soft, acid water or slowly conditioned to hard water. Seldom bred in the U.S. but frequently bred in Europe. Most specimens sold in the U.S. are imported from Europe because collecting them is illegal in most states where they occur.

Lepomis macrochirus

BLUEGILL

Eastern U.S.; 6 in.

This species has spread to many areas in Central and southern Europe. A hardy but not particularly colourful coldwater fish.

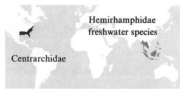
Hemirhamphidae freshwater species
Centrarchidae

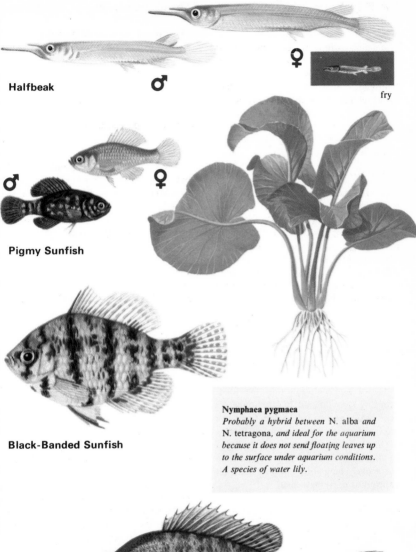

Halfbeak ♂ ♀

fry

♂ **Pigmy Sunfish** ♀

Black-Banded Sunfish

Nymphaea pygmaea
Probably a hybrid between N. alba *and*
N. tetragona, *and ideal for the aquarium
because it does not send floating leaves up
to the surface under aquarium conditions.
A species of water lily.*

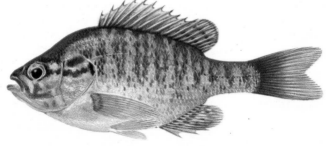

Bluegill

FAMILY CENTROPOMIDAE

This family, which was previously called Ambassidae, consists mainly of salt and brackish water species, distributed in the Indo-Pacific area. Only a small number have found their way into fresh water and very few are common aquarium fishes.

Chanda ranga

INDIAN GLASSFISH

India, Burma, Thailand; in nature 3 in., much less in the aquarium.

This fish is well known to aquarists under the name *Ambassis lala,* but as in so many other cases, this had to be changed when an older and therefore more valid name was found. The glassfish is the only member of the family that has become widespread in aquaria. It is very attractive, and despite its delicate appearance is quite hardy. It thrives best with other quiet fishes in a well-lit tank at 64–77°F. In nature the species often occurs in brackish water and it likes the addition of a small amount of salt (one teaspoonful per gallon of water). It eats only live food. Breeding is not difficult, but the young are very small and require the very finest live food; infusorians are not sufficient. During the first few days the breeding tank should be filled with live food, since the young do not actively hunt food but only eat what happens to move past them.

Chanda buruensis

This species is more elongated than *C. ranga,* and it can be kept and bred in the same way.

Gynochanda filamentosa

Malaya; 2 in.

A very elegant and quite hardy species but one which is only rarely imported. The female lacks the greatly elongated fin rays of the male. It has been bred a few times, but the young do not seem to develop the long fins of the imported fish.

FAMILY UMBRIDAE

A small family with three species in North America and one in South-east Europe, presumably the remains of a larger continuous distribution area.

Umbra krameri

Danube region, South-eastern Europe; ♂ 3½ in., ♀ 5 in.

This little fish is known in central Europe as Hundsfisch (dogfish) because, when swimming, it moves the pectoral and ventral fins alternately like a dog swimming. It is a very sluggish fish, but it occasionally dashes to the surface to obtain air. The female makes a nest in dense vegetation where it guards the eggs and young. The slightly larger fry are cannibalistic if they are not separated. The American species, known as mudminnows, are *U. pygmaea, U. limi* and *Novumbra hubbsi.*

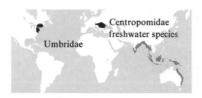

Centropomidae
freshwater species

Umbridae

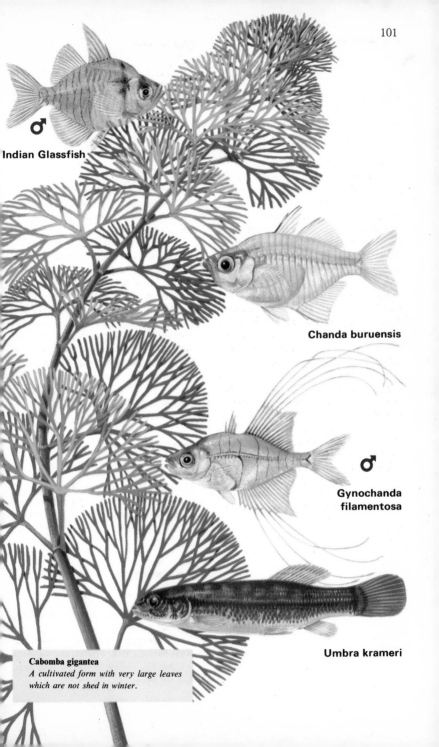

101 de la page.

Indian Glassfish ♂

Chanda buruensis

Gynochanda filamentosa ♂

Umbra krameri

Cabomba gigantea
A cultivated form with very large leaves which are not shed in winter.

FAMILY CICHLIDAE

CICHLIDS

A family containing several hundred species distributed throughout tropical South America, Central America and Africa, together with two species in India. The cichlids are closely related to the perch family, from which they can be distinguished, among other characters, by the presence of only one nostril on each side of the head. In nature most of the species live in slow-flowing or standing waters and take up territories, which means that they are often aggressive towards other members of their own species. This, together with the large size of many species and a propensity for digging in the bottom and eating the plants, accounts for the limited popularity of some cichlids as aquarium fishes. In a correctly furnished special tank, however, they can give more pleasure to the aquarist than any other group of fishes. This is mainly because of their extremely interesting behaviour. Pairs of cichlids often stay together for a long time, and most species practice brood protection, the eggs being deposited on plants or stones, where they are guarded by one or the other parent; in some cases the eggs are incubated in the mouth of the parent. The young are also protected from predators until they become large enough to fend for themselves. The larger cichlids should, without exception, be kept in special tanks.

Cichlasoma

This South American and Mexican genus contains large, aggressive species which give much pleasure and are easy to keep in a tank by themselves.

Cichlasoma meeki

FIREMOUTH CICHLID

Guatemala and Yucatan; 6 in.

Cichlasoma species are easy to breed. The eggs are deposited in a pit dug by the parents in the bottom sand and are protected against attack. If a large brood is wanted, the young can be removed after hatching, but occasionally, one should allow a brood to remain under the care of the parents to enjoy watching them look after their progeny. Not only are predators chased away, but the school of young fish is carefully kept together. Any that stray are gently taken into the mouth of one of the parents and spat out into the middle of the school. The young of large cichlids can eat the finest dry and live food immediately after hatching.

Cichlasoma festivum

FESTIVUM

Guyana and the Amazon Basin; 6 in.

A peaceful but shy fish which stays among dense vegetation. It is, however, difficult to breed.

Cichlasoma nigrofasciatum

ZEBRA OR CONVICT CICHLID

Guatemala, San Salvador, Costa Rica, Panama; 4 in.

Although not very colourful, this is one of the hardiest of the cichlids and it spawns readily. The female is smaller and paler than the male.

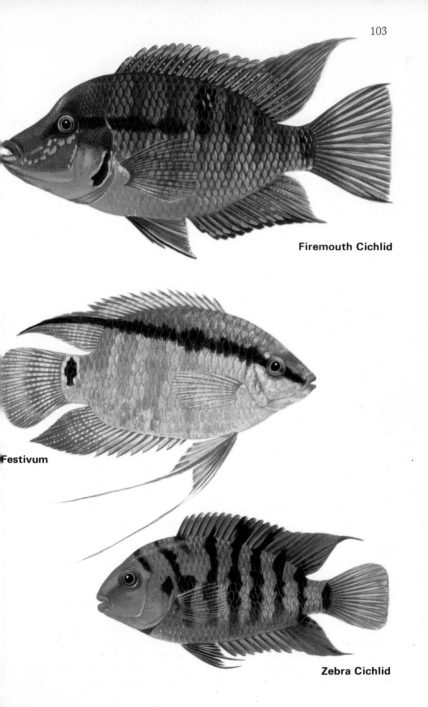

Firemouth Cichlid

Festivum

Zebra Cichlid

Jack Dempsey

Cichlasoma biocellatum

JACK DEMPSEY

Amazon Basin; 7 in. in nature.

An attractive and very popular cichlid. The colours of the female are duller than those of the male. It was named after the famous boxer for a very good reason: it is one of the most aggressive cichlids. Each pair should be kept alone in a large tank.

Aequidens latifrons

BLUE ACARA

Panama and Colombia; 6 in.

A hardy species. The correct name is possibly *A. pulcher*. The smaller and more peaceful related species *A. curviceps* and *A. maroni* are frequently imported.

Astronotus ocellatus

OSCAR OR VELVET CICHLID

Widespread throughout South America; 13 in.

This is one of the cichlids about which the aquarist should be warned. Small young fish, only a few inches long, are often seen in the trade and with their velvety-brown coloration they are very beautiful. Even under restricted conditions they grow and grow, and it may be difficult to get rid of them in a pleasant way. The adults are much paler than the young and have attractive reddish and orange colours. This cichlid is otherwise easy to keep and relatively peaceful, both towards members of its own species and other fishes. A mature pair can be most appealing, after becoming tame enough to enjoy being stroked by a hand.

Nannacara anomala

GOLDEN-EYED DWARF CICHLID

Western Guiana; ♂ 3 in., the female smaller.

This dwarf cichlid is one of the best aquarium fishes in the family. It is peaceful towards members of its own species and other fishes and can therefore be kept in the community tank. It does not stir up the bottom or eat the plants. After mating the male must be removed as the female then becomes very aggressive.

105

Blue Acara

young

Oscar Cichlid

♂ when scared

Golden-Eyed Dwarf Cichlid

♀

♂ at rest

Apistogramma

The South American cichlids in the genus *Apistogramma* are all small and are therefore very popular with aquarists. Some of them are aggressive, however, and the aggressive kind should be kept in a special tank or in a very spacious community tank with several hiding places in the form of tree roots, flower pots, etc. As a rule species of this genus spawn readily.

Apistogramma agassizi

AGASSIZ'S DWARF CICHLID

Amazon region; ♂ 3 in., ♀ 2 in.

This species spawns readily. The dark red eggs are laid on the underside of stones, in as sheltered a position as possible. They are guarded by the female, which at this stage may sometimes become so aggressive that it is necessary to remove the male and any other fishes from the tank. The relatively tiny fry begin to feed about four to five days after hatching and they should be given fine live food. The female cleans the young by putting them in her mouth, 'chewing' them, and then spitting them out again. Strangely enough the broods often contain far more males than females. This species is very sensitive to chemicals in the water, and appears to be susceptible to *Ichthyophonus* infections.

Apistogramma reitzigi

YELLOW DWARF CICHLID

Rio Paraguay Basin; ♂ 2 in., ♀ smaller.

Care and breeding as for the preceding species.

Apistogramma borelli

BORELLI'S DWARF CICHLID

Matto Grosso; ♂ 2½ in., ♀ smaller.

Not a very widespread species. The older males develop elongated dorsal fin rays. In the very similar species *A. trifasciatum,* the male has a rounded caudal fin. These two species are often confused with each other and with the rarely imported *A. ortmanni* and *A. cactuoides.*

Microgeophagus ramirezi

RAMIREZ'S DWARF CICHLID OR RAMIREZI

Venezuela; 2 in.

In the literature this species is often called *Apistogramma ramirezi* as it resembles this genus in appearance. It can, however, be distinguished by a number of points; it does not, for example, hide its eggs, but deposits them out in the open; the two sexes are almost identical, and the species is monogamous, whereas *Apistogramma* species are polygamous. These characters have justified the establishment of a separate genus for this beautiful and popular dwarf cichlid. This is a good example of how the behaviour of a fish can sometimes be used in systematic zoology.

This species is very easy to keep but rather difficult to breed.

Ramirez's Dwarf Cichlid

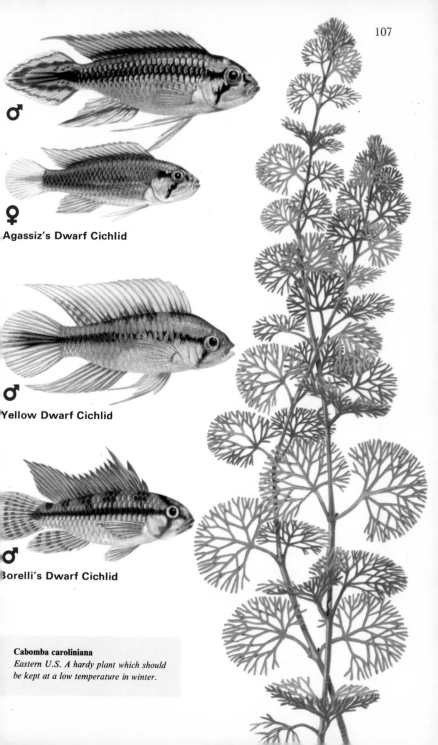

107

♂

♀

Agassiz's Dwarf Cichlid

♂

Yellow Dwarf Cichlid

♂

Borelli's Dwarf Cichlid

Cabomba caroliniana
*Eastern U.S. A hardy plant which should
be kept at a low temperature in winter.*

Pterophyllum scalare

SCALARE OR ANGELFISH

Amazon and Rio Negro Basins and Guyana; up to 6 in. long and 10 in. high.

This is undoubtedly the most common cichlid in aquaria, and this is largely because of its striking appearance and hardiness. It does not attack the plants or other fishes and can therefore be kept in the community tank, but is really at its best when kept with members of its own species in a separate large tank. There are no external differences between the sexes.

The angelfish is not particular about temperature or type of water, but may be rather fastidious about food; it prefers a varied diet of live food. For many years breeding was very difficult, but this is no longer so. It is best to allow the breeding fish to choose their mates from a group of young individuals. The eggs are laid on broad leaves or pieces of flat stone and they and the newly hatched fry are guarded by the parents. The mature eggs are 'chewed' by the parents and this releases the young, which are then spat out on to a surface. Later, they may be moved to a pit in the gravel where they are also guarded, and they now begin to take the finest live food. The eggs should be removed from the parents before hatching if one wishes to breed on a large scale. During mating and territorial fights the male may emit a rumbling sound.

The name *P. eimekei*, which is often used in aquarium literature, is an invalid synonym of *P. scalare*. The genus contains two other species, *P. altum* and *P. dumerilii*, which are almost identical with *P. scalare*. They are only imported very rarely and appear to be very delicate. They have not been bred in the aquarium.

In recent years several different 'improved' forms of *P. scalare* have appeared on the market, of which the most popular have been the charcoal-coloured or black forms and those with long, veil-like fins, or those with a combination of both these characters. The black forms, in particular, are more delicate than the wild type.

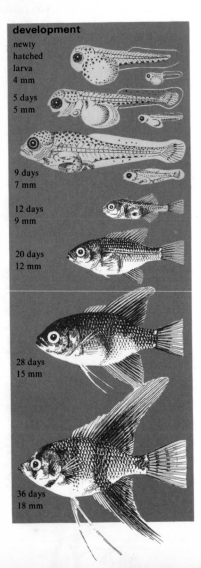

development

newly
hatched
larva
4 mm

5 days
5 mm

9 days
7 mm

12 days
9 mm

20 days
12 mm

28 days
15 mm

36 days
18 mm

Angelfish

Veiltail form

Black form

Vallisneria gigantea
New Guinea. A hardy plant, with leaves up to 40 in. long, which requires plenty of nutrient.

Discus

Symphysodon

The discus fishes in the genus *Symphysodon* form a small group of two species (one with three subspecies) of colourful, elegant and very desirable large cichlids. They are difficult to keep, difficult to breed and difficult to import from the places where they are caught, and for these reasons really fine specimens command high prices.

In nature they occur mainly in small watercourses with clear, soft brown water with a low pH and a high temperature.

Although the discus fishes are all peaceful, they should be kept in a separate tank in water with a degree of hardness not exceeding 5 DH and for spawning a pH of 5·5–6·0. Many aquarists recommend frequent changes of the water, up to a third of the volume per week. The tank should be densely planted, as they do not damage the plants like other cichlids and their often marked nervousness is reduced if the tank also has dark hiding-places. Large individuals may panic and damage them-selves, particularly if the light is suddenly switched on or off. It is important to keep them well supplied with a varied diet of live food.

Discus fish are difficult to breed. There is no clear sex distinction and the mating pair must normally be allowed the opportunity to separate off from a large flock of young fishes. The eggs are laid on a solid leaf or stone that has previously been cleaned, and are guarded by the parents until they hatch three days later. The small fry, still with the yolk sac intact, hang for a further three days, during which time the parents move them at regular intervals. When the yolk has been absorbed a new, quite unique phase of parental brood protection begins. Both parents produce a nutritional secretion on the sides of the head and body and the young feed on this. It is only when they are quite large, about half an inch long, that they start to take other food, and they gradually become quite independent of the parents.

The individuals vary a great deal in

Blue Discus

colour pattern and therefore the differences mentioned in the following descriptions may be difficult to see.

The genus contains the following species and subspecies:

Symphysodon discus

DISCUS

Amazon, Rio Negro and Rio Cupai, Brazil; 8 in.

Characterized by the horizontal wavy blue bands on a reddish-brown background, which cover the whole body.

Symphysodon aequifasciata

This species has three subspecies:

Symphysodon aequifasciata aequifasciata

GREEN DISCUS

Amazon region near Sanatarem; 6 in.

Horizontal wavy blue bands on a dark green to brownish-green background. These bands are normally lacking on the central part of the body. In addition there are often nine dark, vertical stripes. Seldom imported.

Symphysodon aequifasciata axelrodi

BROWN DISCUS

Amazon region, Rio Urubu; 5½ in.

A dark brown background, almost without horizontal blue bands. Very frequently imported.

Symphysodon aequifasciata haraldi

BLUE DISCUS

Amazon region; 5 in.

The very distinct wavy blue bands, which are lacking on the central part of the body, make this one of the most attractive and popular of the discus fishes. In addition, it is apparently the hardiest.

Jewel Fish

Hemichromis bimaculatus

JEWEL FISH OR RED CICHLID

Northern tropical Africa; 6 in.

An exceptionally beautiful cichlid. The background coloration may vary somewhat, from bright red to reddish-brown. This cichlid is easy to keep and breed, as the pair take great care of their young. Unfortunately it is extremely aggressive, and must be kept in pairs in a separate tank without plants.

The newly hatched young spend a great deal of time hunting for food outside the mouth of the female. She is able to feed at this stage, but at the slightest indication of danger all the fry seek shelter in her mouth. These mouthbrooding cichlids have been much used as research animals by those studying animal behaviour, because in a limited space and with simple equipment, one can investigate several interesting innate behaviour patterns.

Tilapia mossambica

MOZAMBIQUE MOUTHBROODER

East Africa; 14 in.

This species is sometimes called *T. natalensis*. The females and the young males are an inconspicuous grey colour, but the older males, when ready to spawn, are exceptionally handsome. Fortunately they achieve this beautiful coloration before they are fully grown, when they are only 4–5 in. long. On account of its size, this cichlid is only suitable for a separate tank. The male digs a deep pit before mating, for which purpose its lips become greatly thickened. As soon as the eggs have been laid, the female takes them up into her mouth where they are fertilized. The pair should be separated after mating.

T. mossambica *guarding its young.*

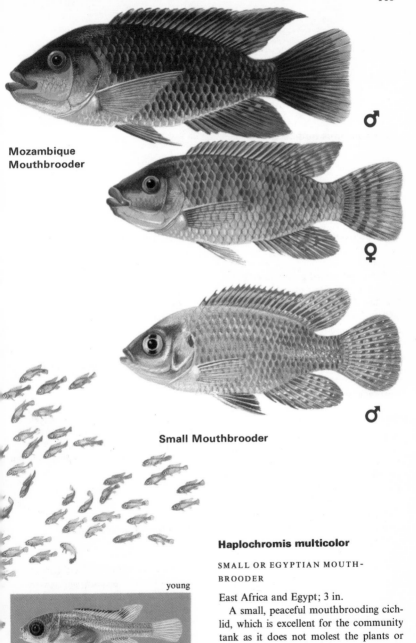

Mozambique Mouthbrooder

♂

♀

Small Mouthbrooder

♂

young

Haplochromis multicolor

SMALL OR EGYPTIAN MOUTH-
BROODER

East Africa and Egypt; 3 in.

A small, peaceful mouthbrooding cichlid, which is excellent for the community
tank as it does not molest the plants or
other fishes. It is also very easy to breed.

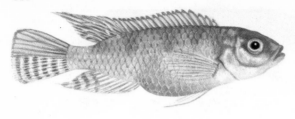

Nannochromis nudiceps

Nannochromis nudiceps

Congo; 3 in.

This dwarf cichlid greatly resembles the species of *Pelmatochromis* and care and breeding are the same as for these. This species can be easily kept in an aquarium with plants, and it prefers soft, slightly acid water at 75–82°F. Unfortunately it is rarely imported.

Pelmatochromis

The West African dwarf cichlids in the genus *Pelmatochromis* resemble the South American dwarf cichlids *(Apistogramma)* in many respects. They are relatively peaceful towards members of their own and other species and are quite gentle to the plants. Some species, however, can dig and so the plant roots should be protected with pots and large stones.

A great many of the species seem to prefer the addition of a small amount of salt, as in nature they are to be found in slightly brackish water.

Pelmatochromis pulcher

Nigeria; ♂ 3½ in., ♀ 3 in.

Sold under the name *P. kribensis*, this is quite a hardy species but it requires warmth. The eggs are laid in a flower pot or other shelter, and both parents take part in brood protection.

In this species the female has the brightest colours.

Pelmatochromis subocellatus

EYE SPOT CICHLID

Gaboon to the mouth of the Congo; 4 in.

A colourful but rare fish which should be cared for in the same way as the preceding species. A number of other *Pelmatochromis* species are imported, but our knowledge of their systematics is, as yet, incomplete.

Pelmatochromis thomasi

Sierra Leone; 3½ in.

Care and breeding as for the preceding species. When *Pelmatochromis* species are kept in a community tank one must expect disturbance on the day when the pair mates. Other fishes are ruthlessly chased away and if the aquarium is not large enough they may even be killed.

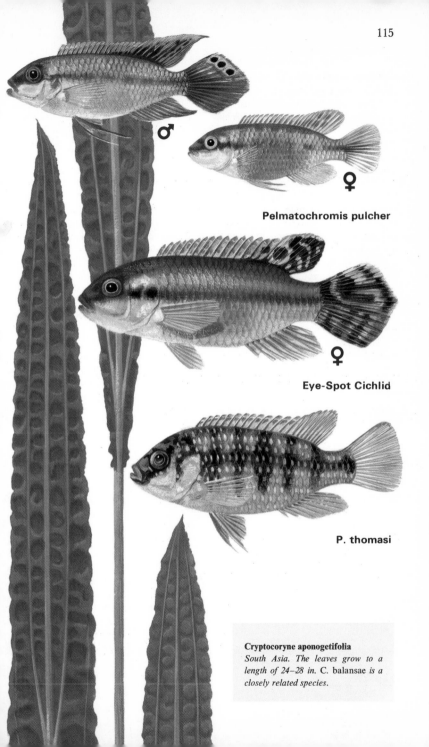

Pelmatochromis pulcher

Eye-Spot Cichlid

P. thomasi

Cryptocoryne aponogetifolia
*South Asia. The leaves grow to a
length of 24–28 in.* C. balansae *is a
closely related species.*

NYASA CICHLIDS

In recent years a number of colourful cichlids have been imported from Lake Nyasa in Central Africa. This lake contains over two hundred endemic cichlid species, i.e. species that are not to be found anywhere else in the world and which have evolved in this lake over a long period of time. Even though Lake Nyasa is very old and has long been isolated from other lakes, so that there has been plenty of time for the evolution of endemic species, it is nevertheless a considerable zoological mystery that so many species have been able to evolve side by side.

Several of the Nyasa cichlids occur in nature in different colour phases. Since the individuals showing these different colours are not geographically separated one cannot call them races, and they have, therefore, no separate scientific name.

All the species seem to be hardy and to spawn readily but they are rather quarrelsome. As far as is known, the imported species all practise brood protection as do most of the other Nyasa cichlids. This is presumably correlated with the very high density of individuals in the lake, as under such conditions mouthbrooding effectively protects both eggs and young from the pursuit of other cichlids.

Labeotropheus fulleborni

5½ in.

The thick upper lip and thin, chisel-shaped teeth of the *Labeotropheus* species indicate that they are specialized to graze on the thick layer of algae, with its collection of small animals (primarily midge larvae), that grows on the rocky shores of Lake Nyasa. All the males and some of the females are blue with darker transverse bands, but some females are orange with black blotches and spots. Although primarily vegetarian in nature, this species thrives in the aquarium on the normal animal diet given to other cichlids.

Labeotropheus trewavasae

5½ in.

Males and some of the females are pale blue with darker transverse bands and a red-brown dorsal fin. More than half the females, however, belong to a yellowish-brown phase with black blotches and spots, which is very similar to the corresponding phase in *L. fulleborni*.

Pseudotropheus elongatus

5 in.

Like the preceding species this form is to be found foraging on the algae-covered rocks and therefore requires vegetable matter in its diet. There is only one colour phase and the sexes are almost identical, the female being usually a little paler than the male.

In the genus *Pseudotropheus* the lips are not so well developed as in *Labeotropheus,* and the very fine teeth are used for scraping algae and small animals from the rocks.

Labeotropheus fulleborni

L. trewavasae

Pseudotropheus elongatus

Pseudotropheus tropheops

P. novemfasciatus

Pseudotropheus tropheops

5 in.

Although a relatively inconspicuous member of the Nyasa cichlid group, the male in breeding colours is striking, as it then becomes very dark with a brilliant blue spot on each scale. It appears to spawn just as readily as the other species. The young of these Nyasa cichlids can be kept with the adults without being molested, provided the tank is large enough.

Pseudotropheus novemfasciatus

4 in.

This species is very similar to the preceding form but is smaller, and both sexes are reddish-brown with indistinct transverse bands. *P. novemfasciatus* has a tall, rather bulldog-like profile. There is only one colour phase in this species.

Pseudotropheus auratus

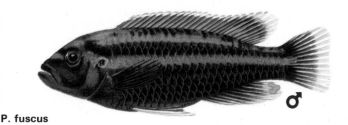

P. fuscus

Pseudotropheus auratus

3½ in.

The dark coloration is usually only shown by the dominant male in a tank, or sometimes by several males, while the other adult males have the handsome golden coloration of the females and the young. Strangely enough, the adult females appear to be able to assume the colouring of the male under certain conditions, but the significance of this is not clear.

Pseudotropheus fuscus

3½ in.

Very similar to *Pseudotropheus auratus,* but deeper in the body and the bright longitudinal bands of the male are a more intense blue than the corresponding bands in *P. auratus.* These two species are probably the most attractive of the imported Nyasa cichlids and they are relatively peaceful.

Pseudotropheus zebra

Lake Nyasa; 6½ in.

The largest of the imported Nyasa cichlids, although it is sexually mature when only 4–5 in. long. Besides the normal type shown here, other colour phases can be found that are uniform pale blue to almost bluish-white. Also, in a few females, yet another phase can be seen, with a number of irregularly distributed and irregularly shaped black and orange blotches. This species is the most abundant of the Nyasa cichlids and is chiefly found near the algae-covered rocks. Like most other Nyasa cichlids, the males have large, clearly marked yellowish-white spots on the anal fin, which are the same size and shape as the eggs of this species. These anal spots play a part in the courtship of these mouthbreeders. After having taken her newly laid but as yet unfertilized eggs into her mouth, the female snaps at these egg-like markings on the male. This stimulates the male to release his sperm into her mouth where it fertilizes the eggs.

Julidochromis ornatus

Lake Tanganyika; 3 in.

The natural conditions of Lake Tanganyika in Africa resemble those of Lake Nyasa in many respects. It is also a very old lake that has been isolated from other lakes for such a long time that an endemic fauna, mainly of cichlid species, has evolved. Many of these endemic cichlids are just as colourful as those from Lake Nyasa, but they are more difficult to import and so are less commonly seen. They will spawn quite readily but are not very productive. The eggs are deposited in a cave and are guarded by the female. *J. ornatus* seems to prefer hard water.

Julidochromis marlieri is a closely related species, but not so attractive.

Tropheus duboisi

Lake Tanganyika; 4 in.

In this species the young fish are exceptionally beautiful, being velvety-black with white spots. Later, the male develops a reddish, broad transverse stripe on the flank. This species is often mistaken for the very closely related *T. moori*, which lacks pale markings on the body.

It is to be hoped that imports from Lake Tanganyika will increase, and that collectors both there and in Lake Nyasa will attempt to export even more of these exciting endemic cichlid species. There are undoubtedly far more species than those already imported that are suitable for aquarium conditions.

The Tanganyika and Nyasa cichlids are often compared with the coralfishes as regards their magnificent coloration. The comparison is probably correct, for in both habitats populations rich in species and individuals occur, which encourages the development of bright colours.

Etroplus maculatus

ORANGE CHROMIDE

India and Ceylon in fresh and brackish water; 3 in.

Both Asiatic cichlids belong to the genus *Etroplus*, but they have not become very widespread as they are not particularly colourful. The smaller, more attractive, and therefore more frequently imported species is *E. maculatus*. It thrives best with the addition of a small amount of salt and at a high temperature.

The other species, *E. suratensis*, reaches a length of 16 in.

Pseudotropheus zebra

Julidochromis ornatus

Tropheus duboisi
young fish

Cryptocoryne beckettii
Ceylon. Formerly known as
C. ciliata.

Orange Chromide

FAMILY NANDIDAE

A family with very few species in tropical South America, Africa and South-east Asia. This is a typical distribution pattern for an ancient family that is receding.

The Nandidae are small, interesting fishes, but because of their greedy, predatory behaviour and shyness they should be kept in a separate tank.

Badis badis

BADIS

Standing waters in India; 3 in.

The most peaceful of the Nandidae, this fish feeds only on the finer grades of live food. It can therefore be kept in the community aquarium where it does not always reveal its interesting character. A single pair kept in a densely planted tank, without other fish, will settle down and the male will show its fantastic ability to change colour.

The female is usually brownish, and convex on the underside.

Badis feeds exclusively on live food and needs plenty of warmth. It spawns readily in crevices and flowerpots, and the male guards both eggs and young.

Polycentrus schomburgki

SCHOMBURGK'S LEAF-FISH

North-eastern South America and Trinidad; $3\frac{1}{2}$ in.

A rather inactive crepuscular or nocturnal fish, not suitable for the community tank. Otherwise it can be kept like the other leaf-fishes, but it is hardier.

From time to time the very similar species *Polycentropsis abbreviata* is imported from West Africa. This fish is unique among the Nandidae, as it builds a bubble-nest.

Monocirrhus polyacanthus

SOUTH AMERICAN LEAF-FISH

Amazon, Rio Negro and Guyana area; 3 in.

An extraordinarily interesting but difficult fish, which should be kept in a tank of its own. It hangs motionless in the water, like a dead leaf and usually head down, lying in wait for its prey which is then engulfed by the enormously expansible mouth. It is best fed on guppies and similar fishes. It has an extremely large appetite and can consume about its own weight in food daily. The tank should be very densely planted and should have slightly acid and very soft water (pH 6–6·5, 2–4 DH).

The eggs are laid on stones or coarse leaves and the newly hatched young are quite large. After a couple of months they begin to attack each other. The young often develop spots resembling *Ichthyophthirius*, but these disappear later.

Cryptocoryne undulata
Ceylon. This species, closely related to C. willisii, *was formerly known as* C. beckettii.

Badis ♂

♀

Schomburgk's Leaf-Fish

South American Leaf-Fish

FAMILY GOBIIDAE

GOBIES

A family with numerous species, characterized by the completely united ventral fins. They occur mainly in sea water in all the coastal regions of the world, but a few species are to be found in fresh and brackish waters. Very few gobies have become widespread as aquarium fishes.

Brachygobius xanthozona

BUMBLEBEE FISH

Sumatra, Borneo, Java, in slightly brackish water; 1¾ in.

In addition to this species, a couple of other, almost identical, small gobies are imported, but they can only be named accurately by an expert. One of them is *B. nunus* which is widely distributed in South-east Asia and Indonesia.

The bumblebee fish thrives best in water to which a little salt has been added. Because of this and its gentle, unobtrusive behaviour, it should be kept in a special tank, and it will then be easy to breed. The large eggs are laid under stones or in a flower pot and the male protects the brood. The young are free-swimming but the adults are bottom-living fishes.

Aponogeton ulvaceus
Madagascar. May grow very large with numerous leaves. It is best kept in soft, slightly acid water.

Bumblebee Fish

Nymphaea rubra
This is the trade name for this small water lily. The first leaves are submerged but later ones grow to the surface.

FAMILY ATHERINIDAE

A family in which most of the species are tropical marine fishes.

Only a few representatives have entered fresh water, chiefly in places such as Madagascar and Australia where true freshwater fishes are rare. Most of the species have two dorsal fins.

Freshwater species

Telmatherina ladigesi

CELEBES SAILFISH

Celebes; 3 in.

An unusually beautiful and elegant fish, well-suited for a large tank with plenty of swimming space. It is hardy, does not require particularly high temperatures and appears to prefer hard, neutral water. The females have short fins.

Breeding sometimes presents problems, but a pair that has begun to mate will often continue to do so daily over a long period. The young take the finest grades of live food.

Pseudomugil signatus

Australia, northern and eastern Queensland; 1¾ in.

A small, peaceful schooling fish.

Melanotaenia nigrans

AUSTRALIAN RED-TAILED
RAINBOWFISH

Eastern Australia, southwards to Sydney, in fresh and brackish waters; 4 in.

A very active and hardy fish which thrives at temperatures down to 64°F. It is sometimes necessary to add salt to the water. In the female the colours are duller than in the male and the dorsal and caudal fins shorter.

Breeding is not difficult, and spawning usually takes place at temperatures of 75–79°F. The eggs adhere to plants and hatch in a week. The young take the finest grades of live food. The parents do not normally attempt to eat the eggs or young.

Melanotaenia maccullochi

DWARF RAINBOWFISH

Northern Australia; 3 in.

Because of its small size the dwarf rainbowfish is more popular and widespread than the preceding species, but it can be kept in the same way. The colours of the female are duller than those of the male.

Bedotia geayi

Rivers near the coast in eastern Madagascar; 3½ in.

A recently imported species which does not appear to be exacting as regards temperature, food – which it prefers to take from the surface of the water – and type of water. It is also easy to breed. The large eggs hatch in six days, and the young then remain near the surface. As soon as the yolk sac has been absorbed, they can be fed on *Artemia*.

Acorus gramineus
Japan. A swamp plant which grows extremely slowly underwater.

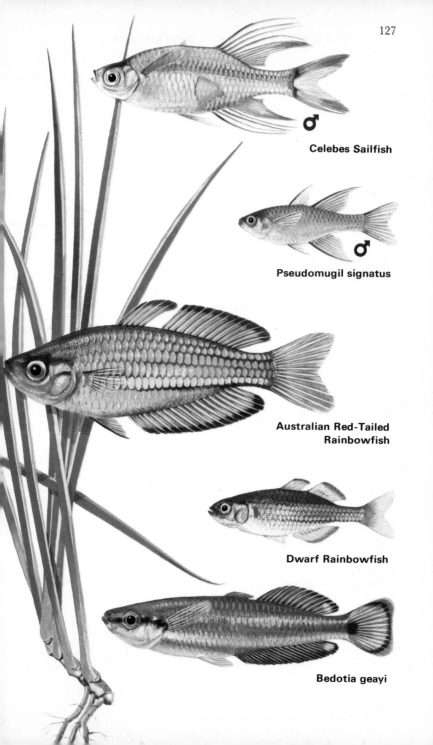

Celebes Sailfish

Pseudomugil signatus

Australian Red-Tailed Rainbowfish

Dwarf Rainbowfish

Bedotia geayi

FAMILY ANABANTIDAE

LABYRINTH FISHES

Freshwater fishes distributed in the tropics
of the Old World, with many genera in
South-east Asia and a few in tropical

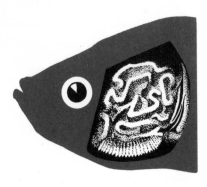

Africa. The popular name of the family
refers to the labyrinth, an accessory
breathing organ. This consists of a cavity
with a number of bony lamellae covered
with a layer of skin which contains
numerous blood vessels. This organ, which
is not developed in the newly hatched
young, extracts oxygen from atmospheric
air which fish take in through their
mouths. They are therefore able to live in
water which has a very low oxygen content
and can often be found in small, very warm
ponds. A few species are able to leave the
pond if conditions are too intolerable and
seek other waters. The gills are poorly
developed and cannot provide the fish
with enough oxygen, even in waters rich in
oxygen, and anabantids therefore die if
they are unable to reach the surface.
Although many of the species should be
kept in tanks of their own, labyrinth fishes
are very popular among aquarists because
they are hardy, beautifully coloured and
are also interesting to watch.

Betta splendens

SIAMESE FIGHTING FISH OR BETTA

Malay Peninsula and Thailand, in standing
or slow-flowing waters; $2\frac{1}{2}$ in.

One of the first aquarium fishes to be
imported and still very popular. One male
or several females may be kept in a community tank. A robust fish, which spawns
readily but is sensitive to temperatures
below 77°F. Like many other labyrinth
fishes the fighting fish builds a bubble-nest.
This consists of air bubbles surrounded by
slime that is so tough as to form a foam
carpet on the surface, in among which the
eggs and newly hatched young are suspended.

The nest is built, guarded and repaired
by the male, which also cares for the young
for the first few days. After three or four
days the male should be removed as it may
otherwise eat the young. These are very
small and must be fed on the finest grades
of live food.

From the relatively drab short-finned
wild type several long-finned forms in a
variety of colours have been bred. These
should be kept in separate small tanks,
arranged so that they can see each other.

Because of the extraordinary comba-
tiveness of the males (they will even attack
their own reflection in a mirror), this
species is used in contests in Thailand.

Various other species of the genus are
imported from time to time, but they are
not so colourful as the domesticated forms
of *Betta splendens*.

Myriophyllum brasiliense
*South America to southern North
America. Requires plenty of light and
in winter a resting period at low temperature.*

129

Siamese Fighting Fish ♀

♂

domesticated forms

♂

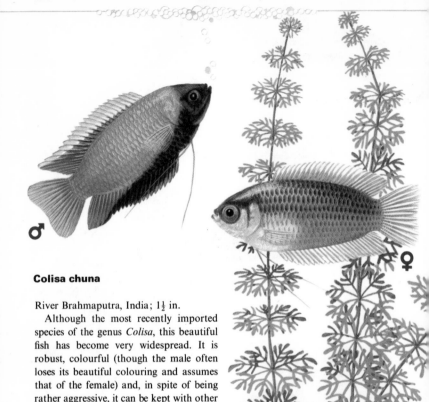

Colisa chuna

River Brahmaputra, India; 1½ in.

Although the most recently imported species of the genus *Colisa*, this beautiful fish has become very widespread. It is robust, colourful (though the male often loses its beautiful colouring and assumes that of the female) and, in spite of being rather aggressive, it can be kept with other fishes in a community aquarium.

It does not appear to require any special type of water, and a pair will readily spawn in a well planted aquarium kept at a high temperature. The bubble-nest is quite small and the parents do not eat the young.

Colisa lalia

DWARF GOURAMI

India; Ganges, Jumna and Brahmaputra river systems; 2 in.

The female is considerably paler than the male and has more rounded fins. This was one of the first labyrinth fishes to be imported and perhaps the most beautiful and peaceful. It only thrives in a densely planted aquarium with plenty of algae, and

Limnophila heterophylla
South Asia. A hardy and decorative plant, usually known as Ambulia.

in this environment it should breed very readily. The male will often chase and eventually kill the female after mating unless they are in a large tank (30 gallons) with plenty of hiding places.

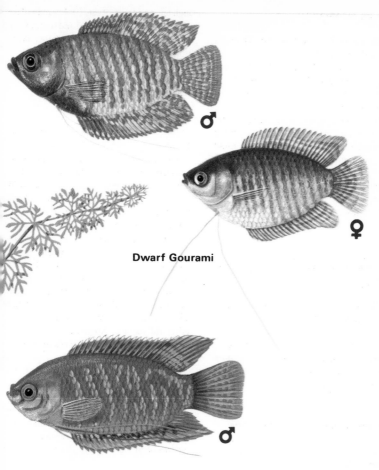

Dwarf Gourami

Giant Gourami

Colisa fasciata

GIANT GOURAMI

East coast of India and in the lowlands around the Ganges and Brahmaputra, North-eastern India and East Pakistan, also in Burma; 4½ in.

This species resembles *C. lalia* but is larger and more aggressive. The female is not so brightly coloured as the male. Care and breeding as for *C. lalia*.

A few years ago *Colisa labiosa* was imported from southern Burma; it reaches a length of 3 in. For many years a subspecies of *C. fasciata* was known by this name.

The male of *C. labiosa* has thicker lips than the male of *C. fasciata* (hence the name). Care and breeding are the same as for the other members of the genus.

132

Trichopsis pumilus

South Vietnam, possibly also Thailand
and Sumatra; 1½ in.

An elegant small labyrinth fish which
requires high temperatures (81–86°F) and
prefers soft water and a bottom of
sphagnum moss.

This species makes a croaking sound
during mating. At this time the level of the
water must be lowered and the tank should
have a number of fine-leaved floating
plants, as the bubble-nest is often placed
among these. Sometimes the pair may even
spawn directly on to the bottom of the
tank. The few eggs hatch in thirty-six
hours.

Trichopsis vittatus

TALKING OR CROAKING GOURAMI

Thailand, South Vietnam, Malay Peninsula, Indonesia; 2½ in.

To be cared for as the previous species.
They appear to mate most readily in
spring, in a thickly planted, sunlit aquarium. Like the previous species, this fish
also makes a croaking sound while mating.

Sphaerichthys osphromenoides

CHOCOLATE GOURAMI

Sumatra, Malay Peninsula; 2½ in.

No clear difference between the sexes.
This very beautiful species is often imported and is greatly sought after. It is
peaceful and interesting, but unfortunately
most imported specimens are extremely
delicate. They are susceptible to various
diseases, particularly white spot *(Ichthyophthirius)* and can seldom tolerate the
various cures for these infections. Therefore, only the experienced aquarist should
attempt to keep imported specimens.
However, once they have become established they are quite hardy, particularly if
kept in soft, slightly acid peaty water at a

high temperature (79–86°F). The chocolate
gourami is difficult to breed and the number
of young is low. Unlike most other labyrinth fishes it is a mouthbreeder.

Helostoma temmincki

KISSING GOURAMI

Malay Peninsula, Thailand, Indonesia;
12 in.

This rather large, coarse and not very
colourful species is imported in two
different colour phases: the so-called wild
type, which is silvery-green with faint
longitudinal stripes, and an almost uniform whitish-pink form. It is not clear
whether they are geographical races or
simply variants. The wild type is rarely
seen in aquaria. The kissing gourami is not
difficult to keep but is rarely bred by
aquarists, perhaps because of its large size.
The eggs are laid directly into the water
and because they are very light they float
up to the surface. Apparently the parents
do not look after them at all, and they do
not build a bubble-nest.

The kissing gourami is so named because two fish will often 'kiss' each other,
and they also touch other objects and
other fishes with their lips. The object of
the touching activity is to scrape off algae,
but the exchange of 'kisses' appears to be
a form of threat display.

Trichopsis pumilus

Cryptocoryne blassi
*Thailand. A hardy and
decorative species.*

Talking Gourami

Chocolate Gourami

Kissing Gourami

Pearl Gourami

Trichogaster leeri

PEARL GOURAMI

Malay Peninsula, Thailand, Sumatra, Borneo; 4½ in.

A fully-developed old male of this species is one of the most magnificent aquarium fishes to be found, with its beautiful colours and elongated fins. In addition to these attributes the pearl gourami is very peaceful, even towards smaller species.

The female is duller than the male and has a silvery breast and throat and shorter fins.

Although like all the labyrinth fishes this species is best kept in a tank of its own, it can also give much pleasure to the observer when kept in a community aquarium, provided the water temperature is sufficiently high. The pearl gourami builds a large bubble-nest and may lay up to two thousand eggs.

The related moonlight gourami, *Trichogaster microlepis,* from Thailand (6 in.), is a peaceful and hardy fish requiring high temperatures, and it should be treated like the preceding species.

Trichogaster trichopterus

THREE-SPOT GOURAMI

Malay Peninsula, Thailand, South Vietnam, Indonesia; 6 in.

A rather inconspicuous species which is occasionally found in aquaria. The popular blue gourami is known as *T. trichopterus sumatranus,* but it is not clear whether this is a subspecies occurring naturally in Sumatra or whether it is a chance mutant which has arisen among aquarium fishes in Indonesia. It is more beautiful and far more widespread in the aquarium world than the wild form.

In addition, there is another form of this species on the market, which is called *Trichogaster* "Cosby". This is a domesticated variant which cannot be given a proper scientific name. It is named after an American breeder, and is often incorrectly spelt as Crosby.

Both the wild and the domesticated forms are easy to keep and are very easy to breed, even for beginners.

From time to time the very large species *Trichogaster pectoralis* (10 in.) is imported.

Three-Spot Gourami

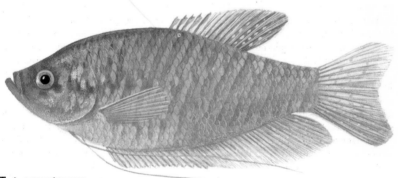

T. t. sumatranus

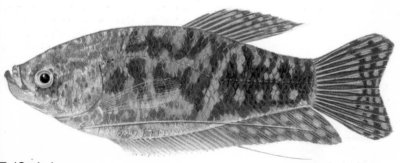

T. 'Cosby'

Macropodus opercularis

PARADISE FISH

Korea, China, South Vietnam, Formosa;
3½ in.

The female is paler than the male and has shorter fins. A very hardy fish, requiring little space; it thrives even in a small tank at temperatures from 59°F, although it needs 68–77°F for spawning. It is not suitable for the community aquarium as it can be very aggressive towards other species.

The paradise fish was one of the first aquarium fishes to be imported and has been kept for centuries by the Chinese. It was probably imported from time to time by ships' captains. As early as 1665, Samuel Pepys gave an account which suggests that the paradise fish was at that time kept in what we would now describe as an aquarium tank.

In many ways the paradise fish is the ideal fish for beginners: it is hardy, colourful, will feed on all types of food, and is exceptionally ready to spawn if kept under reasonable conditions.

The paradise fish is also well known for its ability to rid an aquarium of planarians.

Whereas *M. opercularis* is a fish which also occurs in the wild, the occasionally imported *M. concolor* is most probably a domesticated form.

Macropodus cupanus dayi

BROWN SPIKE-TAILED PARADISE FISH

Southern India, Burma and South Vietnam; 3 in.

A smaller and more elegant species of paradise fish, which is hardy but needs more warmth. The female is distinguished from the male by its shorter fins.

Ctenopoma fasciolatum

BANDED CLIMBING PERCH

Congo Basin; 3 in.

Most of the African labyrinth fishes belong to the genus *Ctenopoma*. Several species are regularly imported but they have not become very widespread in aquaria because of their aggressive, predatory behaviour and their often inconspicuous appearance. Otherwise, these are hardy fishes and are relatively easy to breed. The small species build bubble-nests, some of the larger species are probably mouthbreeders, and others simply lay the eggs in the water and leave them to float up to the surface.

The species shown here is one of the most beautiful in the genus and is also one of the few in which the male has elongated dorsal and anal fins. It builds a bubble-nest.

The *Ctenopoma* species deserve more widespread attention and study among aquarists. They should all be kept in separate tanks, and the larger species should be fed on small fishes, which they stalk in the manner of a pike. One species, *C. oxyrhynchus*, resembles a dead leaf and behaves in the same way as the leaf-fishes.

Cardamine lyrata
East Asia. A cold-water plant, also known as Nasturtium japonicum.

137

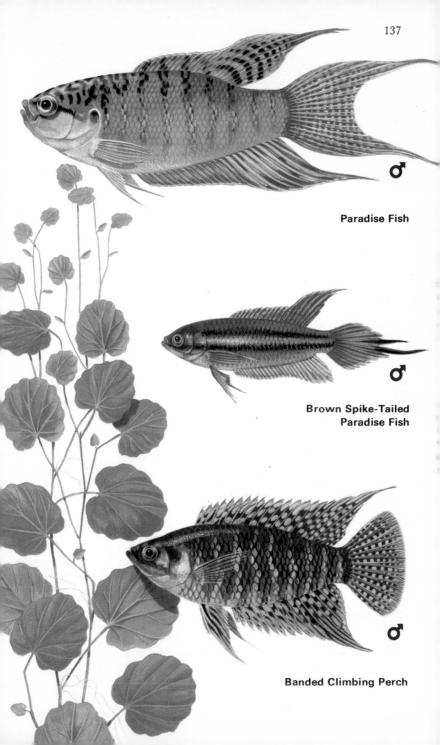

Paradise Fish

Brown Spike-Tailed Paradise Fish

Banded Climbing Perch

Green Pufferfish

FAMILY TETRAODONTIDAE

PUFFERFISHES

A family within the suborder Plectognathi (meaning 'fused-jawed'), the other members of which live in the sea. Pufferfishes occur in fresh and brackish waters in the tropics and subtropics, as well as in the sea. Four teeth form a sharp 'beak' with which the fish can crush hard mollusc shells. All the members of this group swim rather slowly with spiralling movements of the pectoral, dorsal and anal fins and they can puff themselves up with water or air if they are molested. Several members of the family are imported regularly and the small freshwater species are amusing aquarium fishes.

A few species have been bred in captivity. During mating two males attach themselves by their teeth to the underside of a female. Some species appear to practise brood protection.

Tetraodon fluviatilis

GREEN PUFFERFISH

In fresh and brackish waters from India to the Philippines; 8 in.

The most commonly imported puffer-

fish, but not the best suited to the home aquarium. If it thrives it quickly becomes too large and to a greater extent than the other species it seems to require the addition of salt to the water when it reaches a certain size. It has been bred several times.

Tetraodon palembangensis

Thailand, Sumatra, Borneo, in fresh water; 8 in.

A beautiful and frequently imported species which is peaceful although, like the other pufferfishes, it may bite the fins of other fishes. It sometimes also damages the leaves of the aquarium plants.

Carinotetraodon somphongsi

Thailand, in fresh waters; 2½ in.

A newly imported species which has already become widely distributed among aquarists because of its calm and peaceful behaviour and the beautiful colours of the male. The female is a duller mottled brown, without the brilliantly coloured fins of the male. This species has recently been placed in a separate genus because it has a ventral and a dorsal ridge, shown by the male during threat display.

Tetraodon palembangensis

Carinotetraodon somphongsi

Female and two males during mating.

Sagittaria subulata v. pusilla
America. An underwater plant.

BRACKISH-WATER FISHES

The great majority of fish species live either in fresh or salt water and only a few in brackish water. In the tropics most of the brackish-water fishes are associated with river mouths and lagoons where some species, as they grow and mature, wander from fresh water out into the sea or vice versa, only to make the return journey in order to spawn. Others spend their whole lives in brackish water and are often subject to great fluctuations in salinity.

The mangrove swamp is a plant community found in many places where the coast is low and sheltered. Here, mud from the rivers is deposited because of the weaker currents, so that the bottom becomes soft and rich in nourishment, and both salinity and temperature fluctuate considerably on account of the strong ebb and flow of the tides, which alternately cover the area in river water and sea water.

Large parts of the mangrove swamps are above water at the lowest ebb, but only a few highly specialized fishes, such as mudskippers, can remain there under these conditions, the others moving out with the ebbing water. The fauna in such places is poor in species but rich in individuals, and only a few brackish-water fishes have become popular in the aquarium. They are sometimes so tolerant that they can be kept in either salt or fresh water.

FAMILY TOXOTIDAE

ARCHERFISHES

This small tropical fish family, which contains five species distributed in the Indo–West Pacific area, belongs to the perch group.

Toxotes jaculator

ARCHERFISH

Coasts and river mouths from the Red Sea to Australia; 8 in.

No external sexual differences. In nature the archerfish is found in fresh, brackish and sea water. But it is not to be found far up the rivers or far out to sea, and is primarily associated with brackish water in mangrove swamps, estuaries, etc.

The archerfish is renowned for its method of hunting, for it obtains a considerable proportion of its food by shooting down flies, grasshoppers and other insects from leaves above the surface of the water. From below the surface, the archerfish can, with great accuracy, squirt a jet of water or a number of drops for a distance of up to five feet. The mechanism of this unique weapon is quite simple. In the roof of its mouth the archerfish has a groove which forms a tube when the fish closes its mouth. This tube works like a rifle barrel and the power to shoot comes when

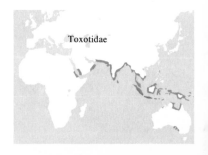

Toxotidae

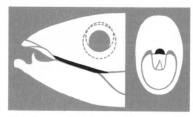

The palate in archerfish. Vertical longitudinal and transverse sections.

the gill-covers are suddenly compressed so that some of the water that is present in the gill cavity is squirted forward at high speed. The drops hit the insect with such force that it loses its footing and falls into the water, where it is immediately snapped up.

In a large, correctly furnished special tank, this fish is hardy and very interesting, but it requires plenty of heat (77–82°F). It can be kept in fresh, brackish or salt water. Most enjoyment is obtained if the aquarium is high and only partly filled with water so that flies can be introduced into the section above the water. Archerfish can also be trained to shoot down chopped meat which is placed on the glass, and will also eat other dead and live food like other aquarium fishes. There should be hiding places in the aquarium, as they can be very timid. They have never been bred in captivity.

Archerfish

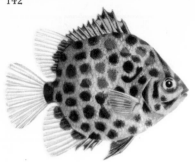

Scat or Argus Fish

FAMILY
PERIOPHTHALMIDAE

MUDSKIPPERS

A small tropical fish family belonging to the goby group. A number of species in a few genera, all distributed in tropical, brackish-water, coastal areas of the Old World.

FAMILY
SCATOPHAGIDAE

A small group of coastal fishes from South-east Asia, north Australia and parts of the West Pacific. The name *Scatophagus* means 'dung-eater' and these omnivorous fishes are often to be found near sewer outlets and in other badly polluted areas.

Scatophagus argus

SCAT OR ARGUS FISH

Coastal waters in South-east Asia, Indonesia and Australia; in nature up to 12 in.

This brackish-water fish is frequently imported and the very beautiful young (about $1\frac{1}{4}$–$1\frac{1}{2}$ in. long) are often bought by aquarists, in spite of the fact that they cannot be kept satisfactorily in an ordinary aquarium. Scats grow rather large, and only the young can be kept in fresh water. Later on, some salt must be added, and they can also be kept in pure sea water. It has never been possible to breed these fish. In one attempt to breed them in sea water the female laid eggs in a cleft in a rock. The so-called *S. rubrifrons* is merely a colour phase of *S. argus*.

Periophthalmus koelreuteri

MUDSKIPPER

Widely distributed in the tropical coastal areas of the Old World, but the exact distribution of this species cannot be given as the systematics of the genus have been very poorly investigated; 6 in.

Mudskippers are found almost exclusively in mangrove swamps, shallow areas near river mouths and in lagoons where the salinity fluctuates greatly. They are sometimes to be found so far up the rivers that the water is quite fresh, but they do not, however, live entirely independent of brackish-water areas.

The mudskipper is one of the few fishes that can leave the water. Of course it must constantly keep the skin and gills moist, but it can be observed to skip and crawl many yards away from the water up into a bush or across dried mud flats. Its permanent abode may be a stone or a root, from which it can survey its territory. At low tide it digs burrows down to the water. Prey and rivals are pursued over land in a series of long leaps.

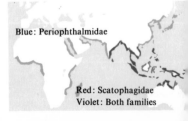

Blue: Periophthalmidae

Red: Scatophagidae
Violet: Both families

Mudskippers are sometimes imported but have not become widespread, as they cannot be kept with ordinary aquarium fishes. They require a special tank arranged as a vivarium with a few inches of water and several rocks, tree roots or sandbanks extending above the water, and with warm, humid air.

They can be kept in fresh, brackish or pure sea water and are very hardy, although individuals sometimes engage in violent territorial fights. They will eat both live and dead food, which should be placed on land. When properly kept they are exceptionally lively and interesting, but they have never been bred. Very rarely, members of the closely related genus *Boleophthalmus* are also imported.

Mudskipper

Pistia stratiotes
Circumtropical. A large floating plant which requires plenty of light and a high humidity.

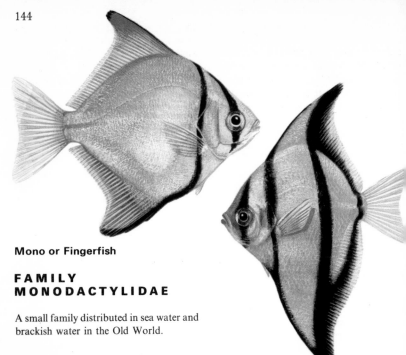

Mono or Fingerfish

FAMILY MONODACTYLIDAE

A small family distributed in sea water and brackish water in the Old World.

Monodactylus argenteus

MONO OR FINGERFISH

River mouths and coastal areas from the east coast of Africa to the West Pacific; 8 in.

Juveniles are frequently imported. With their shining colours and lively behaviour, a school of fingerfishes is a beautiful sight in a large freshwater aquarium, although they really do not belong there. In nature this fish breeds in the lower reaches of the rivers, but the young soon make their way down to the sea, and in the fresh water aquarium the fingerfish does not thrive after reaching a certain size. It then needs the addition of salt, and is really best kept in pure sea water.

The dark stripes on the head and forepart of the body become paler with age. Given a large, open, swimming area and a relatively high temperature they are easy to keep, but have not yet been bred in captivity.

Monodactylus sebae

Coastal districts of West Africa from Senegal to Congo, chiefly in lagoons and estuaries; 8 in.

Imported much less frequently than *M argenteus,* which is a pity, as this is a more elegant species which seems to thrive much better in pure fresh water. Older individuals usually retain the dark stripes. Breeding has not been observed.

Monodactylidae

MARINE FISHES

In tropical marine aquaria, the fishes are almost exclusively chosen from the tropical coral reef. These are colourful fishes that need little space, in contrast to the free-swimming oceanic species.

The coral reef forms a barrier or fringe along certain tropical coasts where the water has a constant salinity and high temperature (never below 70°F, preferably above 76°F), plus a high oxygen content (from much water movement). Here, the living corals are close to the surface as they live in symbiosis with unicellular plants which need light in order to live and grow. In addition to corals, enormous numbers of other lower animals are to be found, of which many owe their existence to the reef. Of all known animal communities, the coral reef is the richest in species and individuals.

Distribution of coral reefs.

Most coral-reef fishes have fixed hiding places and refuges in the reef, and are territorial and often quarrelsome towards members of their own species.

The fishes in this section have been chosen from the many imported species on account of their hardiness and suitable size. The imported fishes belong to several different families, so that often only one representative of each family is mentioned, and no family description is given in this section.

Most marine fishes are widely distributed, as water temperature is the only natural limiting factor. However, fishes living off the coast are often limited to one continent. The term 'Indo-Pacific' in connection with the distribution of many of the species mentioned here, refers to the tropical coasts of the Indian Ocean, the western part of the Pacific Ocean and the oceanic islands, but not normally the Pacific coast of America.

Lutianus sebae

EMPEROR SNAPPER

Indo-Pacific; more than 36 in.

This magnificent fish does not become nearly as large in captivity as it does in nature, even when kept in large tanks, but only very young specimens can be kept by the private aquarist. It is robust, relatively peaceful towards other fishes of the same size, omnivorous and very greedy, so that it unfortunately grows rapidly. In nature the snappers occur in large schools, in contrast to many other coral-reef fishes.

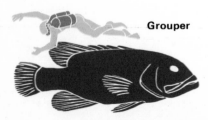

Grouper

Serranus scriba

BANDED SEA-PERCH

Mediterranean, Black Sea and Atlantic coasts of southern Europe and Africa; 10 in.

Although most marine aquarium fishes come from the coral reefs, the Mediterranean Sea also contains a number of suitable species. These have not become so popular as the coral-reef fishes because they are not so colourful, and, paradoxically, they appear to be more difficult to import as there are not so many professional dealers in the Mediterranean. It is therefore usually much easier to procure the true coral-reef fishes. On the other hand, some aquarists may have a chance to catch young Mediterranean fishes while on holiday.

S. scriba lives amongst rocks overgrown with algae, sometimes in quite shallow water, and, with a little luck, it can be caught. It is rather aggressive towards members of its own species, but is usually quite hardy.

Grammistes sexlineatus

SIX-LINED GROUPER OR
GOLDEN-STRIPED GROUPER

Indo-Pacific; 10 in.

A reasonably hardy species well-suited to the marine aquarium, especially when young. In spite of its name, the number of lines varies from three to nine; the number increases with age, and the individual lines are sometimes broken up into white spots, especially in the juveniles.

Small fry of the tropical groupers *Epinephelus* and *Promicrops,* are sometimes imported. Some species can reach a length of over nine feet and are often more feared by divers than are the sharks.

Emperor Snapper

Banded Sea-Perch

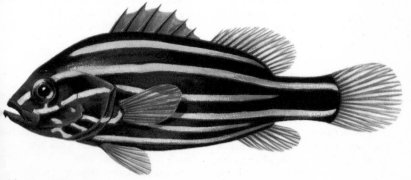

Six-Lined Grouper

Caranx speciosus

Caranx speciosus

Indo-Pacific; 24 in.
  Only suitable for large tanks.
  Quite hardy, but with very delicate skin.

Gramma hemichrysos

Caribbean Sea; 2½ in.
  Imported under the name *G. loreto*.
This brilliantly coloured species is rather
expensive and is at first difficult to keep
but once it has settled down it is quite
hardy. It almost always swims close to
rocks, corals, etc., with its underside
towards them, so that it often hangs per-
pendicularly or back down in the water. It
feeds chiefly on small live food.

Apogon nematopterus

PYJAMA CARDINAL FISH

Celebes, New Guinea; 3 in.
  Not very brightly coloured, but a
beautiful and elegant species, which spends
most of its time hanging motionless in the
water. Not difficult to keep.

Apogon maculatus

FLAMEFISH

Brazil to Florida; 3½ in.
  This is another cardinal fish which is
small enough for the aquarium. It is quite
hardy, in spite of its delicate appearance
and nervous disposition. The genus *Apogon*
is sometimes known as *Amia*.

Eques lanceolatus

JACKKNIFE FISH

Caribbean Sea to Florida; 12 in.
  A very remarkable and elegant fish,
well-suited to the aquarium when young.
It is much sought after, but is unfortunately seldom imported into Europe. A
couple of other species of the same genus
are sometimes to be found, but they do
not have such well developed fins.

Myripristis murdjan

Indo-Pacific; 12 in.
  This handsome soldierfish with large
eyes is in constant movement and is
therefore only suitable for a large tank. It
must never be kept with fishes that are
much smaller than itself as it is very
predacious. In other respects it is easy to
keep.

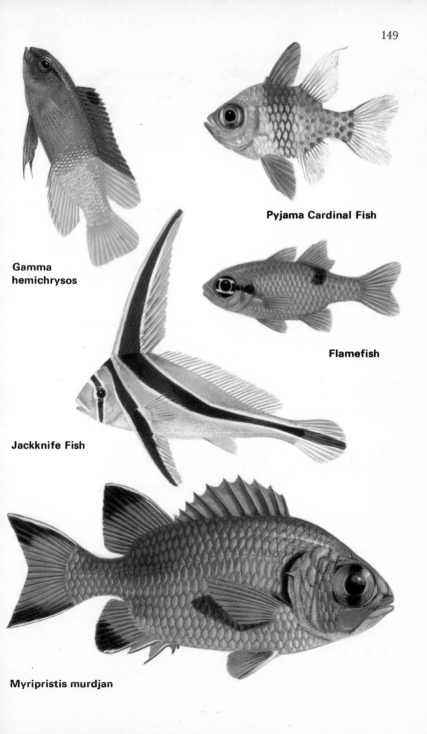

Pyjama Cardinal Fish

**Gamma
hemichrysos**

Flamefish

Jackknife Fish

Myripristis murdjan

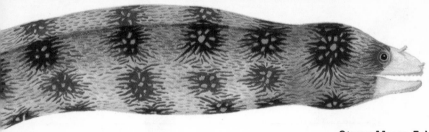

Starry Moray Eel

Echidna nebulosa

STARRY MORAY EEL

Indo-Pacific; 30 in.

It is unlikely that the moray eels will ever become popular aquarium fishes, for they are much too aggressive, not only towards other species but also towards the aquarist, and they hide themselves away a great deal. Small specimens, however, are interesting and are occasionally imported. They may be rather fastidious about food, but once a suitable diet has been found they are hardy. They are best fed on fish cut into pieces of a suitable size, strips of pig's heart, shrimp, etc., offered on forceps. *Muraena helena* from the Mediterranean, which may reach a length of over three feet but is not particularly colourful, is often imported, and so are several very beautifully coloured species from the tropics.

Plectorynchus orientalis

ORIENTAL SWEETLIP

Indo-Pacific; 16 in.

The sweetlips in the genera *Plectorynchus* and *Gaterin*, which should possibly all go under the latter name, include several species the systematics of which are extraordinarily confused. Not only do individuals within a species vary a great deal, but each individual undergoes a complete change in coloration during the course of its life. *P. orientalis* has longitudinal stripes when it is fully grown. When young they are very suitable for the aquarium, but as adults they become too restless and bulky. The young have a peculiar wriggling method of swimming, which is, incidentally, seen in many other marine fishes.

Heniochus acuminatus

PENNANT CORALFISH

Indo-Pacific; 8 in.

Regularly imported, sometimes when only half an inch long. These fry may be delicate and difficult to rear, but slightly larger specimens are robust. They are also peaceful towards each other; so they can be recommended as among the best coral-reef fishes for the private aquarium.

Zanclus cornutus

MOORISH IDOL

Indo-Pacific; 8 in.

One of the most magnificent and most sought-after of all coral-reef fishes. Very difficult to transport, so most of the newly arrived specimens are in poor condition and very susceptible to disease. Because of the small mouth they can only feed on very small live and dead food. The individuals are usually intolerant of each other. They prefer a spacious, light aquarium with plenty of swimming space.

The so-called *Z. canescens* is probably only a juvenile form of *Z. cornutus*.

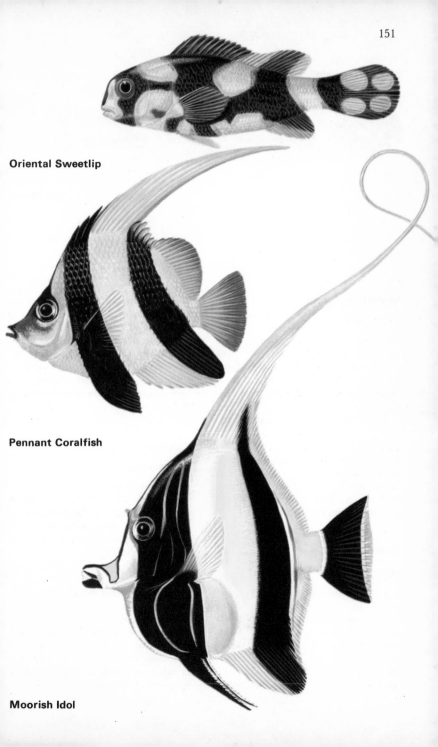

151

Oriental Sweetlip

Pennant Coralfish

Moorish Idol

Red Mullet

Mullus surmuletus

RED MULLET

Mediterranean, Eastern Atlantic Ocean and North Sea; 14 in.

Red mullet are found in shallow water where they often swim around in schools testing the sea bed with their feelers for anything edible.

This is one of the many beautiful and interesting Mediterranean fishes, but is not easy to keep. It is very fastidious about food; chopped shrimp and small earthworms appear to form a suitable diet. From time to time, other, even more brilliantly coloured red mullet species are imported from the tropics.

Chelmon rostratus

LONG-NOSED BUTTERFLYFISH

Coasts of South-east Asia to the Philippines; 7 in.

A frequently imported species which may be somewhat unpredictable, in that some specimens thrive while others do not and refuse to feed. The long scissor-shaped snout is used in nature to suck small animals, such as crustaceans, out of

holes. This and the following species can often be induced to feed by offering *Tubifex* or whiteworms which have been allowed to hide in coral stems or the like, so that each worm has to be sucked out. Later the fish learn to take the more usual kinds of food. It is usually impossible to keep several specimens of this species in the same tank.

Forcipiger longirostris

FORCEPS FISH

Indo-Pacific; 8 in.

This species is even more specialized than the previous one for sucking small animals from their holes. It is very difficult to keep, susceptible to disease and fastidious about food.

Chaetodontoplus mesoleucus

Indo-Pacific; 5½ in.

Although more closely related to *Pomacanthus* than to members of the genus *Chaetodon*, this species resembles the latter in appearance and, to some extent, in behaviour. It is rather difficult to keep.

Long-Nosed Butterflyfish

Forceps Fish

Chaetodontoplus mesoleucus

Chaetodon vagabundus

C. octofasciatus

C. ocellatus

C. melanotus

Chaetodon

MARINE BUTTERFLYFISHES

The genus *Chaetodon* contains a large number of species distributed in all the tropical seas of the world, and especially in the Pacific and Indian Oceans. Most of the species have beautiful markings and brilliant coloration, and as they are also of moderate size they are frequently imported. In nature they live singly or in pairs, each within its own territory. This territory is fiercely defended, primarily against members of its own species, and as a marine aquarium is never large enough to allow the establishment of more than one territory, it is not usually possible to keep several specimens of the same species together. On the other hand, one can sometimes keep a few specimens of several different species in the same tank, as species of very different appearance do not normally attack each other.

Chaetodon species are extremely popular among aquarists, but they cannot be regarded as fishes for the beginner. Many specimens are delicate, and it is often difficult to obtain newly imported fishes which are in good enough condition to be capable of fighting infectious diseases. They should be fed mainly on live food and are very sensitive to excess nitrate in the water.

Very little is known about the behaviour of the different species in aquaria, so the methods of caring for each species cannot be given, and the species shown here are therefore not dealt with individually.

All the species illustrated are from the Indo-Pacific area, except *C. ocellatus* and *C. capistratus* which come from the West Indies. Several other species are imported.

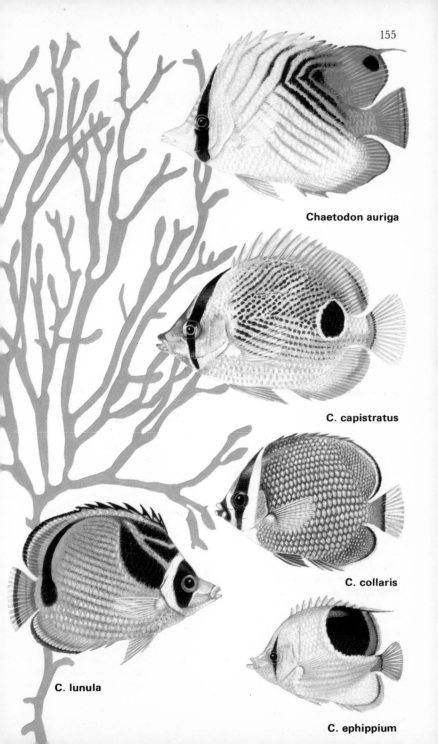

Chaetodon auriga

C. capistratus

C. collaris

C. lunula

C. ephippium

young

adult

Imperial Angelfish

Pomacanthus imperator

IMPERIAL ANGELFISH

Indo-Pacific; 14 in.

The imperial angelfish is quite exceptionally beautiful, especially when young but, like so many other coral-reef fishes, its appearance changes radically with age. As young fishes they are eminently suitable for the larger type of marine aquarium, but are unfortunately rather expensive. In addition to this species, the true imperial angelfish, the young of two other closely related species, *P. semicirculatus* and *P. annularis,* are also imported from the Indo-Pacific area. These require exactly the same aquarium conditions as the true imperial angelfish but they are usually cheaper and just as beautiful. In the young of *P. semicirculatus* the pale lines at the base of the tail form a semicircle, whereas in *P. imperator* they form a closed circle, and *P. annularis* has vertical pale transverse bars on a dark blue background. The adult fishes of the three species are also rather different: *P. annularis* develops pale stripes which run diagonally from the head up towards the tip of the dorsal fin, while *P. semicirculatus* becomes a uniform yellowish colour.

Pomacanthus arcuatus

FRENCH ANGELFISH

West Indies; 14 in.

Holacanthus tricolor

ROCK BEAUTY

Caribbean Sea; 24 in.

A very striking and quite hardy species. In the adult the edges of the dorsal and anal fins are red, but this characteristic marking seldom develops in the aquarium.

157

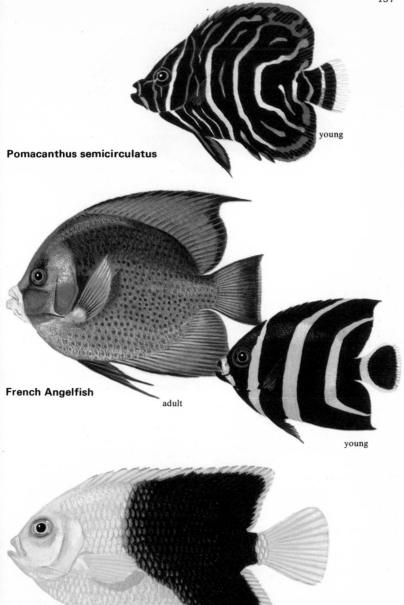

Pomacanthus semicirculatus

young

French Angelfish

adult

young

Rock Beauty

adult

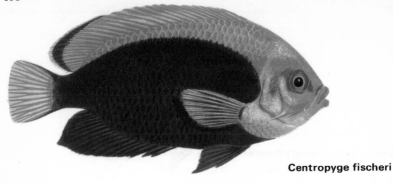

Centropyge fischeri

Centropyge fischeri

Indo-Pacific; 3 in.

The species of *Centropyge* are closely related to the imperial angelfish and are popular with aquarists because of their small size and bright coloration. They are hardy but very aggressive towards members of their own species.

Pomacentrus melanochir

Pacific Ocean; 2¾ in.

The family Pomacentridae (damselfishes) includes some of the most suitable fishes for the marine aquarium. They are generally small, colourful, easy to care for and feed, and because, in nature, the young live in large schools, they are often tolerant towards members of their own and other species. In addition, they are free-swimming, active fishes which show themselves in an aquarium, and they are also frequently imported at a reasonable price. As adults they sometimes become intolerant of members of their own species.

The striking contrast of the blue body and the yellow tail in *P. melanochir* becomes less striking with age and in adults both colours are less intense than in the juveniles.

Chromis caeruleus

BLUE PULLER

Indo-Pacific; up to 5 in.

An attractive species, varying from pale green to pale blue, which is peaceful and easy to keep.

Chromis chromis

Mediterranean Sea and Atlantic coasts of South Europe and North Africa; 4 in.

A hardy aquarium fish, well-known as being exceptionally tolerant to a high nitrate content in the water. The juveniles are a brilliant blue.

Abudefduf oxyodon

Indian Ocean; 4½ in.

This is one of the most attractive species in the genus *Abudefduf*, which is widely distributed throughout the whole Indo-Pacific area. *Abudefduf saxatilis*, the Sergeant Major, is yellowish with five dark transverse stripes.

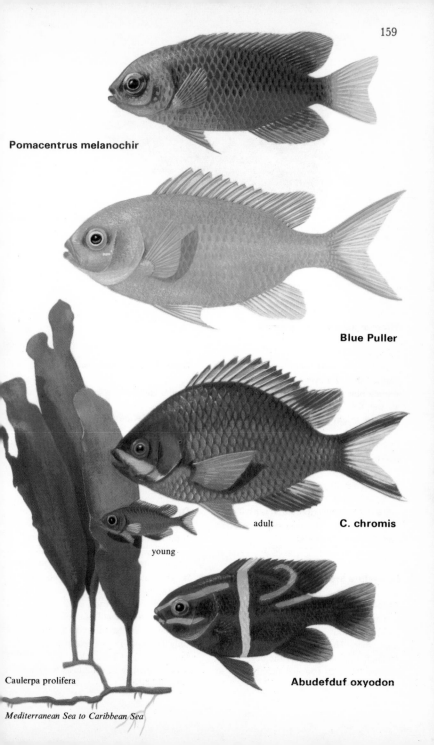

Pomacentrus melanochir

Blue Puller

adult   **C. chromis**

young

Caulerpa prolifera

Mediterranean Sea to Caribbean Sea

Abudefduf oxyodon

Microspathodon chrysurus

Microspathodon chrysurus

Caribbean Sea; 6 in.

One of the most beautiful West Indian damselfishes, but very quarrelsome. The shining blue blotches disappear gradually as the fish grows, but the caudal fin becomes bright yellow.

Dascyllus reticulatus

Indo-Pacific; 2¼ in.

A fish with rather subdued colours, which is regularly imported. It is hardy and easy to keep. *D. marginatus* and *D. carneus* are very similar.

Dascyllus aruanus

Indo-Pacific; 3½ in.

The young are often imported at a length of about an inch, and at a reasonable price. This is one of the best and hardiest marine fishes for the beginner. It is peaceful, even towards members of its own species.

Dascyllus melanurus

Pacific and eastern Indian Ocean; up to 2¾ in.

Resembles the previous species in general appearance and behaviour, but differs in the pattern on the dorsal and caudal fin. It is just as frequently imported.

Dascyllus trimaculatus

Indo-Pacific; 4 in.

A fine, velvety-black fish with three white spots, which is often imported and is very hardy. The bright contrast in coloration fades with age. The young are peaceful towards each other and should be kept in a small school. They later become quarrelsome and the adults can only be kept singly even in a very large tank. Like the Clownfishes, the fry of this species can live in symbiosis with certain sea-anemones.

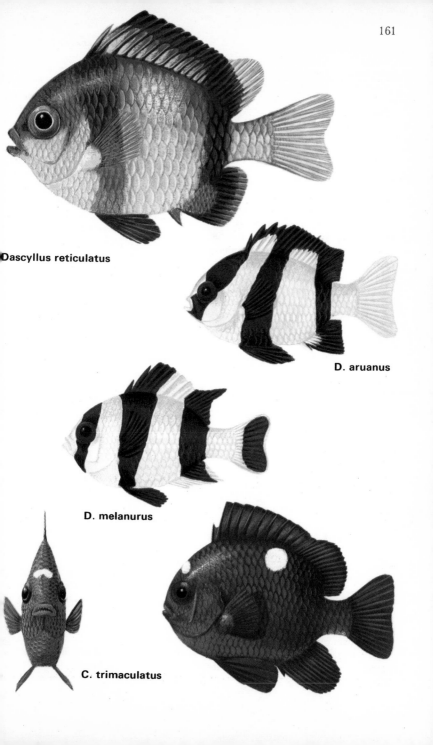

Dascyllus reticulatus

D. aruanus

D. melanurus

C. trimaculatus

Indo-Australian area; 6 in.

Closely related to the Clownfishes mentioned below, but with a sharp spine behind the eye.

Amphiprion percula

CLOWNFISH

Pacific and eastern Indian Ocean; 3 in.

The most frequently imported and one of the most beautiful of the genus. The Clownfish is an excellent fish for the beginner, being reasonably priced, fairly hardy and attractive. It becomes quite easily accustomed to taking fine dead food. Small individuals should be fed several times a day to obtain satisfactory growth. Like all clownfishes it swims with characteristic wriggling movements.

Amphiprion sebae

Sumatra to East Africa; $4\frac{1}{2}$ in.

Care as for the preceding species, but it is hardier.

Amphiprion xanthurus

East Africa to the Pacific coast of Japan; 3 in.

Resembles *A. sebae*, but is darker, and sometimes almost black.

Amphiprion bicinctus

Indo-Pacific; $4\frac{1}{2}$ in.

The extent of the transverse bar in the middle of the body is variable. Young specimens have traces of a third bar at the base of the caudal fin.

The clownfishes in the genera *Amphiprion* and *Premnas* are well known for their symbiosis with certain large tropical sea-anemones of the family Stoichactinidae. Normally these sea-anemones feed on fish of about the same size as the clownfish, which they hold and kill with the sting-cells of the tentacles. Clownfish, however, can rub themselves unscathed between the tentacles of the sea-anemone, indeed, in nature they are only to be found in association with a sea-anemone. It is obvious that such an association is advantageous to the clownfish which can retreat in among the tentacles of the sea-anemone on the approach of an enemy. However, the presence of the clownfish is also to the advantage of the sea-anemone, as it has been shown that these fishes actively bring it food and remove foreign bodies.

How does the clownfish avoid being killed and devoured by the sea-anemone? There is no question of immunization against the sting-cells, for these are not released at all, and in fact the tentacles of the sea-anemone do not react as they normally would, i.e. by retracting, when a clownfish rushes into them. It has been shown that the fish become covered by anemone slime and are thus regarded a part of the anemone. Even a dead clown fish does not release the sting-cells, unless its skin is damaged. On the other hand, a clownfish which has had the slime removed from its skin is immediately attacked and probably killed. However, there is some indication that this skin secretion is not always present. In some *Amphiprion* species it has been shown that if they are kept for a long time without sea-anemone they may be killed when they are then put together with one. But only a few days pass before the surviving fishes have 'learned' to associate with the sea-anemone. It is believed that the sea-anemone in some way stimulates the secretion of the skin slime. The different clownfishes nor

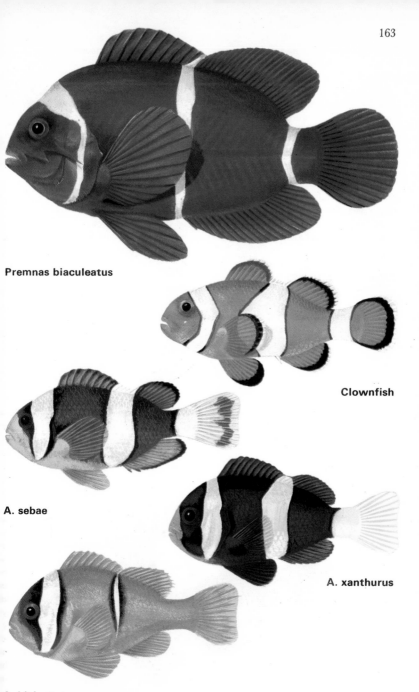

163

Premnas biaculeatus

Clownfish

A. sebae

A. xanthurus

A. bicinctus

164

mally associate with certain definite species of sea-anemone, but they can frequent others.

The fidelity with which the different species of *Amphiprion* associate with sea-anemones varies considerably. In nature *A. akallopisos*, for example, never strays more than an inch or two away from its anemone, whereas a species such as *A. ephippium* seems to be quite independent of its sea-anemone. Aquarium observations indicate that both sea-anemones and clownfishes live longer if they have the opportunity to associate with each other, than if they are kept alone.

Amphiprion laticlavius

Pacific Ocean; 3 in.

A characteristic species with a pale, saddle-shaped dorsal marking.

Amphiprion akallopisos

Indo-Pacific; 4 in.

Amphiprion perideraion

Indo-Pacific; 3 in.

Resembles the previous species, but has a narrow pale stripe running across the gill-cover.

Amphiprion ephippium

Indo-Pacific; 6 in.

One of the most beautiful clownfishes, especially when the diffuse black marking on the flank is fully developed. This does not always happen, however, and many young fish lack this marking which does not always develop when they are reared in an aquarium. Individuals both with and without the white transverse band occur. The presence of this band is often given as a characteristic of the species *A. ephippium*, as opposed to *A. frenatum*, which should lack it. However, the pale band in *A. ephippium* is a character of the young fish and it disappears with age. *A. frenatum* is a similar species which is seldom imported.

Amphripion laticlavius

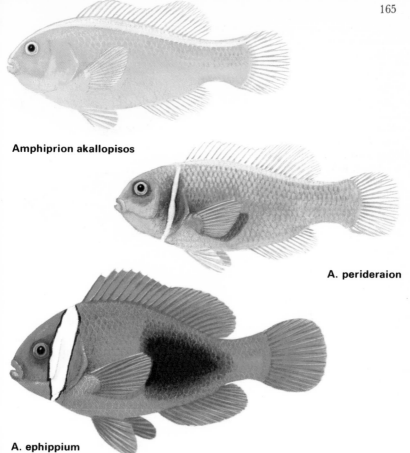

Amphiprion akallopisos

A. perideraion

A. ephippium

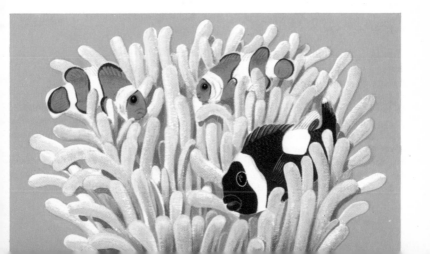

166

Coris julis

RAINBOW WRASSE

Mediterranean Sea and eastern Atlantic
Ocean; up to 8 in.

One of the most attractively coloured
wrasses of the Mediterranean, and well
suited to the larger type of aquarium. This
fish is found in two colour phases: the
large, colourful 'C. julis' form with a red
zigzag band running along the body, and
the smaller, more brownish, so-called 'C.
giofredi'. They were at one time presumed
to be two different species. However, it
has been observed that all individuals
start off with the 'C. giofredi' colouring,
and also that all individuals start life as
females. After a long period as a sexually
mature female, the individual changes to a
functional male and remains so for the
rest of its life. At some stage in the
development, the coloration changes from
the 'C. giofredi' pattern to the 'C. julis'
pattern, but this change does not occur at
exactly the same time as the sex change.
One can, therefore, observe sexually mature
males with the 'C. giofredi' pattern, as
well as sexually mature females with the
'C. julis' pattern.

Coris julis is a hardy species, but the
males are very quarrelsome amongst themselves.

Coris formosa
Coris gaimardi

Indo-Pacific; 16 in.

These two species are only imported as
young fish, and at this stage they are
difficult to distinguish from each other,
and so they are dealt with together here.
In both species the colour pattern of the
young fish is fundamentally different from
that of the adult fish, a phenomenon that
is very common in coralfishes and which
has complicated the systematics of these
fish still further.

The illustration on this page shows the

Coris formosa

Coris gaimardi

difference between the two species when
they are young. When they reach a length
of about 4 in. they start to change to the
adult pattern, which is different in the two
species. Fish in aquaria often retain the
pattern of the young fish all their lives,
possibly because of an inadequate diet.
to keep. The bottom should consist of

These two *Coris* species, with their
brilliant colours and lively behaviour, are
much sought after by marine aquarists.
They are hardy and usually not difficult
fine sand because they dig themselves in at
nightfall, as do the other members of the
genus.

Coris angulata

Indo-Pacific; up to 36 in.

In spite of the large size of the adult fish
this is an excellent aquarium fish since the
imported specimens are seldom more than
2 or 3 in. long and they grow very slowly.
Care as for the two previous species. At the
change over to the adult pattern the large
red markings on the flanks disappear.

Rainbow Wrasse

'julis'

'giofredi'

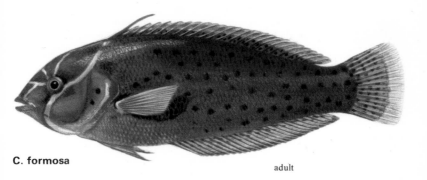

C. formosa

adult

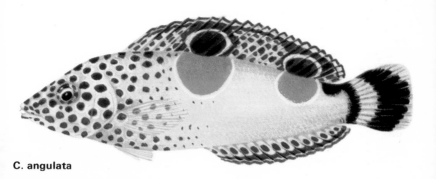

C. angulata

Labroides dimidiatus

CLEANER WRASSE

Indo-Pacific; 4 in.

Cleaner wrasse are characterized by their extraordinary method of feeding. They live chiefly on skin parasites and dead tissue on the skin or on food scraps from between the teeth of other fish, and there is a strange symbiosis between the cleaner wrasse and many species of larger fish. The cleaner wrasses are very stationary; so the large fish come to them and allow themselves to be cleaned, whilst remaining quite motionless in the water. Even fish-eating species will allow the cleaner wrasse to swim into their mouth, into the gill-chamber and so on, and it is thought that the colour pattern and characteristic 'wagging' or wriggling movement of the cleaner inhibits the predatory instinct of the large fish. Observations in the sea have shown that large fish not only actively seek the haunts of the cleaner wrasse, but also, when the spot is occupied by another fish, wait patiently until it is their turn. If the cleaner wrasses are removed from an area, most of the large fish disappear too, and the rest are attacked by parasites, fungi, etc.

In certain areas there are 'false' cleaners, other species which are very much like the genuine ones but do not feed on parasites and are predatory. These false cleaners approach the large fish in the same way, and then suddenly nip off a piece of flesh or gill.

Several other fish species act as cleaners. Of these, many such as the neon goby (p. 181) have the same colour pattern as *Labroides*, while others have different coloration.

One can also observe the behaviour of the cleaner wrasse in the aquarium, even though the fish being cleaned is usually not much bigger than the cleaner. Fortunately, *Labroides* will eat other things besides parasites, and in the aquarium it can be fed on the usual dead and live food.

They appear to be very hardy, although extremely quarrelsome amongst themselves.

Hemigymnus melapterus

Indo-Pacific; 28 in.

Very small young specimens are frequently imported, but it is sometimes difficult to get them into good condition.

Thalassoma lunare

GREEN WRASSE

Indo-Pacific.

Several species of the genus *Thalassoma* are imported. They are extremely hardy and colourful fishes, and even though some grow rather large they do not require a lot of space.

Not all specimens of *T. lunare* are as beautiful as the specimen illustrated, and possibly only the old males have the full coloration.

The species of *Thalassoma* dig themselves into the bottom at night.

Thalassoma bifasciatum

BLUEHEAD

Caribbean Sea, Atlantic Ocean to Florida; 10 in.

In this attractive species the young are a pure yellow and they live as cleaner fish.

Cleaner Wrasse

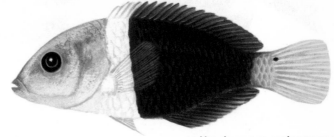

Hemigymnus melapterus

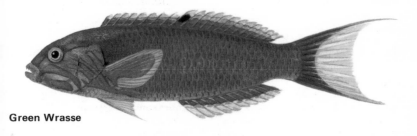

Green Wrasse

Bluehead

young

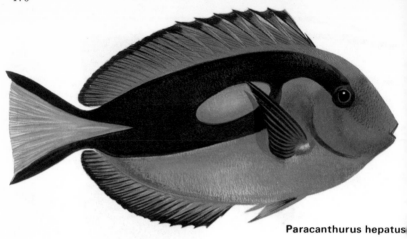

Paracanthurus hepatus

Paracanthurus hepatus

Indo-Pacific; 10 in.

Imported under the name *P. teuthis*, this is one of the most handsome of the coralfishes, but it is unfortunately very expensive and rather susceptible to disease. Once it has become acclimatized it makes an excellent aquarium fish, being active and by no means fastidious about food. The blue colour on the body disappears with age, while the yellow areas spread. The fishes shown on these two pages belong to the so-called surgeonfishes, a name given because of the small, scalpel-shaped spine on each side at the base of the caudal fin. In many species the spine can be depressed into a groove in the flank and when it is raised it is directed obliquely forward. These fish use the spine primarily when fighting amongst themselves, and can inflict serious injury.

Acanthurus leucosternon

WHITE-BREASTED SURGEONFISH

Indian Ocean; 12 in.

This is one of the most frequently imported surgeonfishes. It is quite hardy.

Zebrasoma veiiferum

Indo-Pacific; 12 in.

Although this species is less brilliantly coloured than its relatives, the fins are exceptionally large and when they are raised the fish becomes almost circular in shape. Once acclimatized the young fish are very hardy.

Naso brevirostris

Indo-Pacific; 17 in.

Small specimens are often imported. In the genus *Naso* the caudal spines are immobile.

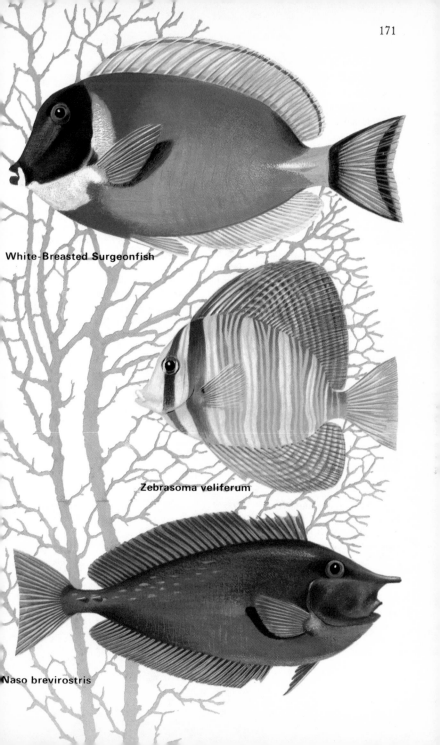

171

White-Breasted Surgeonfish

Zebrasoma veliferum

Naso brevirostris

Odonus niger

Indo-Pacific; 20 in.

A quite peaceful, though rather large triggerfish. It is often possible to keep several individuals together and mating attempts have been observed in the aquarium. The pair dig themselves a pit in the sand like the cichlids. *Odonus niger* belongs among the triggerfishes, so-called because the first and second spiny rays of the dorsal fin form a trigger mechanism. If the first ray is raised it can be locked in position by the second ray so that it is impossible to force it down. In this way, triggerfishes wedge themselves into narrow rock crevices or between coral stems when they wish to hide from enemies. When cleaning the aquarium great care must therefore be taken in removing them from their hiding-places. Some of the genera are also known as filefishes because of the rows of coarse, rough scales at the base of the caudal which are possibly used during fighting.

The triggerfishes belong to the Plectognathi, an order in which the teeth form a very solid gnawing mechanism. In nature these are probably used to scrape anything edible from the corals and rocks.

Rhinecanthus aculeatus

PICASSO FISH

Indo-Pacific and Atlantic coast of Africa; 12 in.

Young specimens about half an inch long are often imported and are now probably the most common triggerfish in aquaria. They are undemanding, but often lose their bright colours in captivity, and are sometimes aggressive towards each other.

Balistapus undulatus

Indo-Pacific; 12 in.

Included as a representative of the many other beautiful triggerfishes that are imported. Small specimens of these species are very suitable for a large marine aquarium.

Oxymonacanthus longirostris

Indo-Pacific; $2\frac{1}{2}$ in.

One of the oddest members of the triggerfish group. The long, trumpet-shaped snout is undoubtedly adapted for sucking corals and other small animals from holes, and in accordance with this the fish moves about quietly, usually head down. In the aquarium, if it can be tempted to eat by offering it *Tubifex* hidden in dead corals, it soon becomes almost omnivorous and seems to be hardy. It is definitely a sociable fish that does not molest either its fellows or other fishes. This is one of the most highly recommended species, but is unfortunately seldom imported.

Oxymonacanthus longirostris

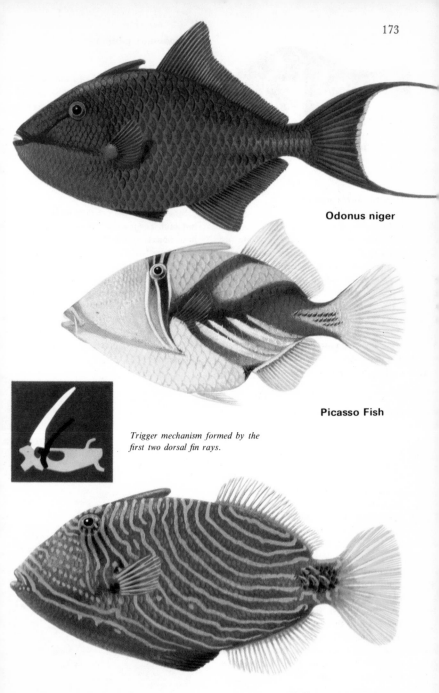

Odonus niger

Picasso Fish

Trigger mechanism formed by the first two dorsal fin rays.

Balistapus undulatus

Canthigaster valentini

Canthigaster valentini

Indo-Pacific; 8 in.

Young specimens 1 or 2 in. long are often imported and are very suitable for marine tanks. All the fishes on these pages belong to the same main group as the pufferfishes which are kept in the freshwater aquarium.

As mentioned on page 138 several of the pufferfishes kept in fresh water can certainly be acclimatized to sea water and are in many ways good, cheap objects for training inexperienced marine aquarists.

Ostracion lentiginosum

BLUE BOXFISH

Indo-Pacific; 8 in.

A representative of the amusing trunkfishes in which the body is surrounded by an armour with holes for the eyes, mouth, fins and anus. These are quiet and often quite robust fishes. Because of their small mouths they eat only the finer sizes of live and dead food. Several species of trunkfishes are capable of secreting a strong poison which kills all the other fish in the same tank. This usually only happens when they are excited, and they should therefore always be transported singly. There is also the risk that a frightened or sick fish may poison the water in the marine tank to the detriment of the other occupants. In this species the back becomes red-brown with age.

Tetrosomus gibbosus

Indo-Pacific; 12 in.

Insignificantly coloured, but with a bizarre triangular shape. This boxfish appears to be both peaceful and hardy and is quite often imported.

Diodon hystrix

PORCUPINEFISH

Tropical seas; 35 in.

Small specimens are very amusing and peaceful. The jaws are specialized to crush hard objects and in the aquarium this fish should be fed on snails, shrimps and, if possible, small crabs.

It is this species that often used to be brought home by sailors in a distended and dried condition as a souvenir.

Porcupinefish

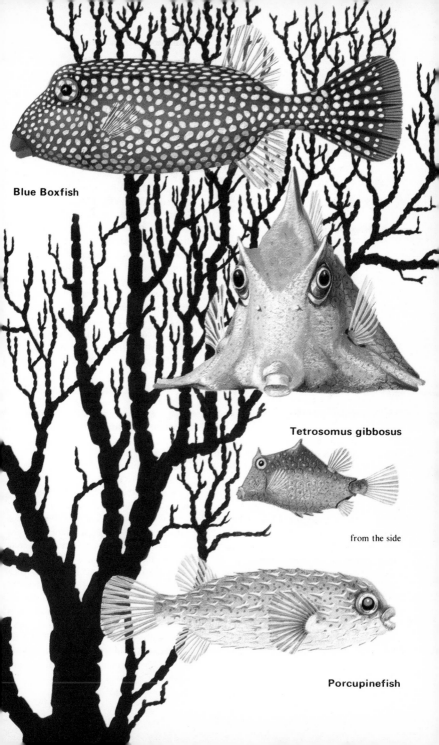

Blue Boxfish

Tetrosomus gibbosus

from the side

Porcupinefish

Opisthognathus aurifrons

Opisthognathus aurifrons

Caribbean Sea and Bermuda, in rather deep water; 3 in.

In nature this beautiful species lives in holes and tunnels up to 12 in. long which it has dug out itself. In the aquarium it will also attempt to dig a similar hiding-place. It is therefore important that the bottom of the aquarium is thick enough for the fish to dig into. A mixture of sand and coral gravel seems to be the most suitable. It spends most of its time in front of its hole, into which it disappears rapidly at the slightest disturbance. It is extremely peaceful towards other fishes, but is more aggressive towards members of its own species. It appears to be very resistant to disease and is easy to feed.

Opisthognathus is a mouthbrooder; it has laid eggs on several occasions in aquaria, but it has never been possible to rear the young.

Pterois volitans

DRAGONFISH OR LIONFISH

Indo-Pacific; 14 in.

Usually imported when only 1 or 2 in. long. These are the most amusing fish one can imagine for the marine aquarium and are very hardy. They have enormous appetites and will sometimes consume male guppies almost as long as themselves. As a result of this, they will unfortunately in a very short time grow too large for a normal-sized tank. The spines of the dorsal fins contain a poison which is used against attacking predatory fishes, and also against the aquarist if the fish is handled too much. But if it is dealt with calmly it never uses its poisonous spines, just as it does not attack other fishes unless provoked. The sting is very painful and is sometimes lethal. Several other, very similar *Pterois* species and also members of the related genus *Dendrochirus* are imported, and when young these are all suitable for the aquarium.

Plotosus lineatus

Indo-Pacific; 28 in.

Imported under the name *P. anguillaris*, *Plotosus* is one of the very few catfishes to be found in the sea. It is very definitely a schooling fish, and in nature schools of several hundred individuals can be seen swimming close together across the sea bed. Their markings make the school seem like a mass of heaving worms. In the aquarium several should be kept together. The young are beautiful and not delicate. When catching them one should take care not to be scratched by the sharp spines of the dorsal fins as such wounds easily become infected and are difficult to heal; these spines contain a poison. As soon as *Plotosus* reaches a certain size, it becomes aggressive towards other fishes.

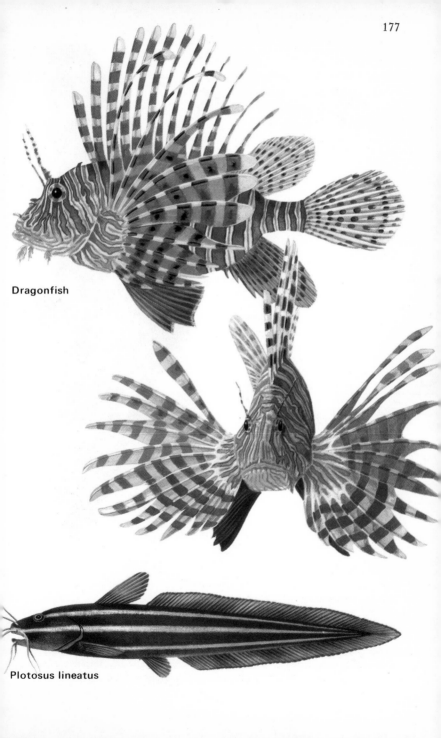

Dragonfish

Plotosus lineatus

Blennius sphinx

SPHINX BLENNY

Mediterranean Sea; 3 in.

The blennies form a family (Blenniidae) rich in species, and are to be found in all the seas of the world. Most of the species are found near the coast, and several live in the small pools left by the receding tide on rocky coastlines. The conditions in these pools vary considerably and are often extreme, and as a result of this, the species one finds in such places are some of the toughest marine fishes of all, capable of enduring incredible fluctuations in temperature (53–104°F in 24 hours), pH and salinity. Like the mudskippers, some tropical species can leave the water and crawl around on the wet rocks, as for instance the East African *Lophalticus kirki*, a rather hardy form. Many species practice brood protection.

Platax orbicularis

BATFISH

Indo-Pacific; 20 in.

As young fishes these are usually very dark and have extremely long dorsal and ventral fins, often relatively longer than those of the best developed veiltail angelfish, but the length of these fins varies considerably. As the batfish grows, the relative fin length decreases, so that the fully developed fish is nearly circular in

P. pinnatus
young fish

shape and an almost uniform silvery-grey. Only young specimens are really suitable for the marine aquarium, and these are elegant and fairly hardy. Because of the very great individual variation, a number of species have been described, but their

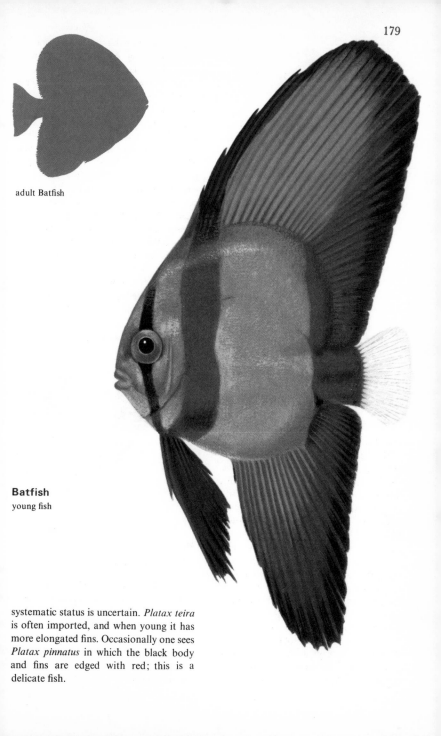

adult Batfish

Batfish
young fish

systematic status is uncertain. *Platax teira* is often imported, and when young it has more elongated fins. Occasionally one sees *Platax pinnatus* in which the black body and fins are edged with red; this is a delicate fish.

The breeding habits of the sea-horse are quite fascinating. After mating the female transfers the fertilized eggs to a brood pouch on the belly of the male. After a period of time the fry hatch, slip out of the pouch and swim straight to the surface. The adults do not pursue them. It is possible to feed the young, but this requires great care and patience. The best food is newly-hatched *Artemia* nauplii, but care must be taken to remove all empty egg-shells, as otherwise the young sea-horses would eat them and subsequently choke. As soon as possible one should start to catch marine plankton to provide the necessary variety to the diet. *Hippocampus guttulatus,* a smaller species from the Mediterranean, is frequently imported. *H. hudsonius,* a large species common along the east coast of the U.S., is frequently kept in aquaria in the U.S.

Hippocampus kuda

GOLDEN SEA-HORSE

Indo-Pacific; 10 in.

The sea-horses are among the most interesting of all fishes, but they are by no means the easiest to keep. They require little space and are very peaceful towards their fellows and other species. The trouble is that they are extremely fastidious about their diet. They feed exclusively on live food, and should be given fairy shrimps *(Mysis)* or other crustaceans of a similar size if they are to thrive. They will eat the larvae of aquatic flies, young guppies and the like, but it is very difficult to keep a sea-horse in good condition on these substitute foods. If *Mysis* are available these fish present no problems, but they should not be kept in the same tank as active, greedy species as they would not get enough to eat.

Hippocampus zosterae

PIGMY SEA-HORSE

West Indies, Gulf of Mexico; 2 in.

This tiny species is often kept by marine aquarists in the U.S., but is unfortunately rarely imported to Europe. The adults thrive on medium-sized *Artemia* and the fry can be easily fed on newly-hatched *Artemia*. This species has been bred for several generations.

Aeoliscus strigatus

RAZORFISH OR SHRIMPFISH

Red Sea to Hawaii; 5 in.

The very compressed body and sharp-edged belly make this one of the most bizarre of all fishes and it is well named razorfish. The way in which it moves is no less extraordinary. Razorfish move about in small schools, each fish standing vertically in the water, head down, and not as is often seen in older publications, with the head upwards. It only assumes a horizontal position when it is necessary to pursue its prey. It looks extremely delicate and is also difficult to transport, but once it has arrived safely at its destination it is amazingly robust. In spite of its small mouth it can take fairly large types of food, such as *Mysis* and *Daphnia*. On the other hand, it is a very slow eater; so it is not advisable to keep it with more greedy species.

Elacatinus oceanops

NEON GOBY

West Indies to south Florida; 3 in.

This beautiful small goby has the same markings as the cleaner wrasse (page 168) and like this fish it obtains its food by cleaning other fishes. Since it is small and beautifully coloured this is an ideal fish for the home marine aquarist. It is even possible to induce it to breed. About a hundred eggs are deposited on a previously cleaned, flattish surface (e.g. the underside of a shell) and these are carefully guarded by the parents. After ten days the eggs hatch, but the parents protect the brood until the fry are quite large.

Lythrypnus dalli

Pacific Ocean off the coast of California, in rather deep water; 4 in.

This species is included as a representative of the colourful tropical gobies. Several species are imported into Europe. They are usually excellent aquarium fishes, although they spend a considerable amount of time motionless on the bottom.

Razorfish

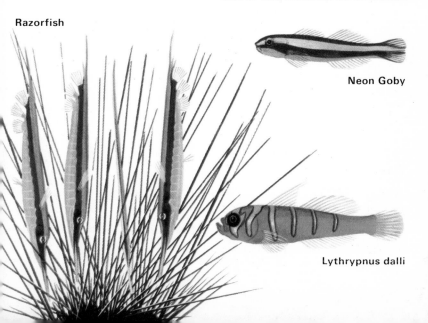

Neon Goby

Lythrypnus dalli

INVERTEBRATES

Enormous numbers of invertebrates are found in the sea, but only a few species have become popular for the marine aquarium. There is no doubt, however, that these groups of animals will become more and more widely known in the future, since so many species are unusual, interesting and very suitable for a medium-sized tank. Unfortunately, many invertebrates are much more delicate than fishes; they seem to be particularly sensitive to pollution by metallic salts and to excess nitrate in the water. In addition, several species are difficult to feed, especially those which feed by filtering organic matter from the water (suspension feeders). In such cases it is possible to simulate conditions in nature by adding pulverized mussel or something similar, and at the same time stopping the filter. The animals then have a chance to extract food from the water for a period of time, before the filter is started up again. Such a suspension of food particles in the water naturally causes an increase in the nitrate content of the water. As an alternative, pulverized food can be carefully introduced around the animal in question with a pipette.

Many invertebrates thrive best when fed sparingly, and it is no advantage to give them all they can consume. This applies especially to sea-anemones, corals and the like. Sometimes stones encrusted with several small invertebrates are sold and these make fascinating objects for study in the aquarium.

Cleaner shrimp

(Stenopus hispidus)

One of the few shrimps regularly imported, this is an attractive but rather delicate animal and the individuals are often aggressive amongst themselves. They feed on small live food and also clean large fishes (see page 168). Many other species of shrimp or prawn make excellent aquarium animals.

Hermit-crabs

Several species of hermit-crabs appear on the market. These are crustaceans in which the hind part of the body is soft and hidden in an empty snail shell. As the hermit-crab grows it has to change to a larger shell; there should, therefore, always be snail shells of a suitable size in the aquarium. Like the true crabs, they feed on all kinds of organic matter and are usually robust and hardy.

Many hermit-crabs live in symbiosis with other animals which sit on their shells, e.g. sea-anemones. When the hermit-crab moves into a new shell it carefully transfers the sea-anemone.

Tubeworms

From time to time the bizarre tubeworms known as sabellids are imported. These have brightly coloured tentacles which catch finely divided organic matter and disappear rapidly into the tube at the slightest disturbance. Some species live buried in the sand; others form calcareous tubes on rocks. They are usually quite hardy in the aquarium.

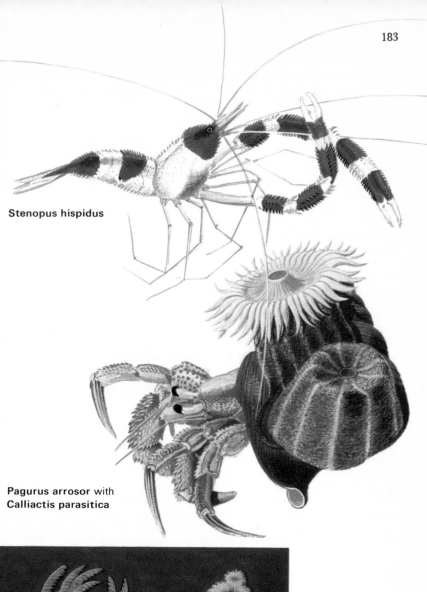

Stenopus hispidus

Pagurus arrosor with
Calliactis parasitica

Tubeworms

Octopus and cuttlefish

Small specimens of octopus (genus *Octopus* and others) are sometimes imported; as the name implies these have eight arms. They require a lot of oxygen and are therefore not easy to transport, but if a specimen survives the rigours of the journey it is usually robust and easy to look after. They feed mainly on crustaceans, particularly crabs, and an octopus can consume crabs as big as itself without being damaged by the claws. In addition many octopuses eat fish but normally they cannot catch fast-moving, healthy fishes in an aquarium.

The octopus is undoubtedly one of the most amusing aquarium animals with its varied, apparently intelligent behaviour and incredible colour changes. Octopuses can become quite tame and will come up to the hand at feeding time, and although their bite is poisonous they very rarely attack humans. Normally it is not possible to keep more than a single octopus in a tank, but if one is fortunate enough to get a pair, they can sometimes be kept together.

From the aquarist's point of view, the greatest disadvantage of octopuses is their large appetite (which causes much water pollution) and the resultant rapid growth. Most species when fully grown are much too large for the home aquarium.

Octopuses have an incredible ability to squeeze through very small holes and cracks; so the coverglass must fit very tightly. They can also lift up the coverglass and escape in this way, so it should be securely anchored.

It is not advisable to stimulate an octopus to eject its ink, as this pollutes the water and also seems to exhaust the animal.

The ten-armed cuttlefishes are more free-swimming than the octopuses and are even more difficult to transport. They are therefore usually only transported as eggs. It is possible to hatch the eggs and rear the young on *Mysis* (fairy shrimp), but because of their need for free swimming space they are usually difficult to keep.

Adult cuttlefishes (genus *Sepia*) live mainly on the bottom.

Horseshoe or King Crabs

HORSESHOE OR KING CRABS

The horseshoe crabs *(Limulus)* are peculiar animals which are found on the Atlantic coast of North America and on the coasts of South-east Asia. They are more closely related to the spiders and the now extinct trilobites than to the true crustaceans.

They are hardy in the aquarium but not particularly exciting to watch. To prevent the water being fouled with food, one can take a *Limulus* out of the tank, lay it on its back and put the food between the legs. It will feed in this position and can then be rinsed clean and put back into the water.

Sea-anemones

Several tropical sea-anemones are imported, including those which live in symbiosis with the clownfishes, and also species from the Caribbean and Mediterranean Sea. In general, they appear to survive the journey very well and to be quite hardy. They are most easily fed with small pieces of fish, mussel, etc., which is placed between their tentacles. They are sensitive to overfeeding and appreciate water movements which will remove slime and waste products from them. Most fishes actively avoid the poisonous tentacles of a sea-anemone, and in a large tank it is possible to keep sea-anemones and fishes together.

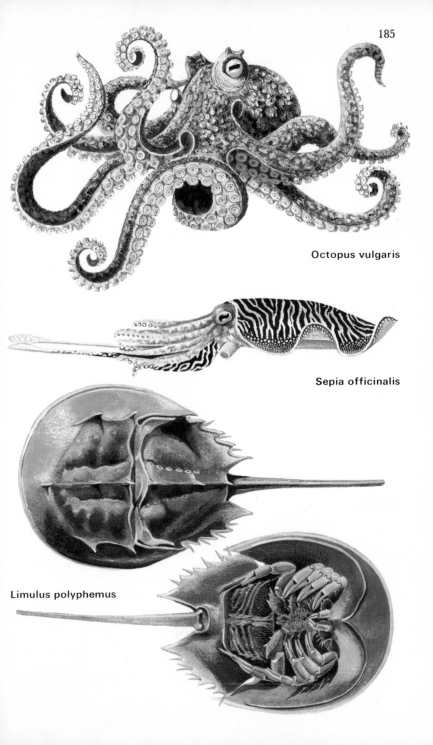

Octopus vulgaris

Sepia officinalis

Limulus polyphemus

PLANTS

The role of plants in the aquarium is chiefly to serve as decoration (in freshwater tanks usually the main form of decoration) and to a lesser degree plants are often sold to help maintain the biological balance by utilizing the harmful metabolic products of the fishes. An essential part of this so-called water-cleansing process performed by the plants is the intake of carbon dioxide which they use in building up new plant tissue, and the output of oxygen; the process is reversed in fishes, for they take in oxygen in respiration and give off carbon dioxide. The assimilation of carbon dioxide by plants takes place solely with the help of light, and therefore only during the daytime in a well-lit aquarium. At other times the plants 'breathe' in much the same way as the fishes, using up oxygen and giving off carbon dioxide. In spite of this, there is no scientific evidence that plants play a really important part in the oxygen

balance of an aquarium. If the tank is in a very light spot and there are only a few fishes in it, one can often see the oxygen bubbling up from the leaves of the plants.

In addition, the plants absorb nutrients (inorganic salts) from the water, which may be derived from decayed food remains and fish faeces; these substances are harmful in large concentrations. But plants only absorb very small amounts of these nutrients and the process is of no real significance in the aquarium.

The extent to which different plants can cleanse the water varies considerably. Some species grow rapidly and need much light and nutrient, but have great cleansing value, others grow more slowly and therefore have neither great cleansing nor oxidizing qualities. The latter, e.g. the species of *Cryptocoryne,* are primarily kept for their decorative value.

If aquarium plants are to thrive, it is important that they have sufficient light. It is not usually possible to illuminate a normal aquarium too brightly for the plants. But, unfortunately, too much light encourages the growth of undesirable algae. With experience the aquarist can determine the right amount of light for plant growth that will not encourage algae. On the other hand, plants which have been growing in a dim light cannot suddenly tolerate brighter lighting; they must first adapt leaf size and the number of chloroplasts to the new lighting.

Aquarium plant culture has been made much more simple in recent years by the development of special fluorescent lights for aquarium use. They are sold under various trade names but all of them emit light in wavelengths that promote growth of the higher plants without encouraging growth of algae. In addition, the plants need a reasonable amount of nutrient, but this will always be present if there are fishes in the tank. It is therefore not necessary to add fertilizer or manure of any kind to an aquarium. Those aquarium plants which absorb nutrients by means of

day   **night**

assimilation

oxygen

carbon dioxide

respiration   respiration

oxygen   oxygen

carbon dioxide   carbon dioxide

nutrient: water and salts

a solid network of roots, as distinct from the floating plants which are merely anchored to the bottom, need a substrate or bottom soil that is coarse enough to permit the movement of oxygenated water between the roots. Only thus can the nutrients reach the roots, and only in this way can they be broken down into a form accessible to the plant. Coarse gravel is therefore far better than fine sand.

Note: *It is well known that bottom filters retard plant growth.*

In the previous pages a total of 53 aquarium plants are illustrated, with brief information on distribution and habitat. For technical reasons it has not been possible to present these plants in the correct systematic order. Therefore, the most important genera are briefly described here.

Acorus

Marsh plants from Asia, which grow very slowly under water, but have great decorative value. Not very demanding as to the type of water.

Anubias

Slow-growing underwater and marsh plants from Central and West Africa. *A. nana* (page 19) has become very popular because of its attractive appearance and small size.

Aponogeton

Widely distributed in the tropics of the Old World, with numerous species. Some of the best aquarium plants belong to this genus, including *A. ulvaceus* (page 124) and *A. crispus* (page 45). The well-known lace

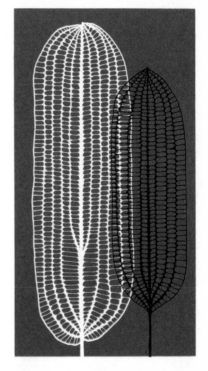

plant *A. fenestralis* lacks tissue between the leaf veins and is a difficult plant to grow as the leaves are likely to become covered by algae, which they cannot tolerate. The new plant lights are a great boon to the lace plant.

The species of *Aponogeton* thrive best in soft, slightly acid water, with a substrate rich in nutrient. Many have an annual resting period when they lose their leaves. The flower grows up above the surface of the water; it is possible to get the seeds to germinate in very shallow water.

Bacopa

Underwater and marsh plants from the tropics of the Old World, which are not much kept in aquaria. The imported species prefer low temperatures, plenty of light and a rich bottom soil.

Cryptocoryne

Asia. This genus includes at least forty species, the systematics of which are very difficult, primarily because they can only

Cabomba

America. These fine-leaved plants are very popular, but tend to lose the leaves on the lower part of the stem. The part which is left with most foliage can then be nipped off and planted as a cutting. *Cabomba* thrives best in soft, slightly acid water. It appears to be sensitive to strong water movements. Like other floating plants it tends to become spindly unless grown in a strong light.

Ceratopteris

Cosmotropical. The only widespread species is *C. thalictroides*, the underwater fern, which, in a well-lit tank, is exceedingly hardy and grows rapidly. It can be grown as a marsh plant, underwater and rooted in the bottom, or as a floating plant.

be identified by the shape of the flower, and aquarium specimens do not often flower unless left undisturbed for many months (perhaps a year or longer). Thus, in the trade newly-imported species often go under incorrect names for many years, until flowering is observed in a botanical garden. Leaf form and size, which are the only characters the aquarist has to go by are often very variable. In nature the species of *Cryptocoryne* are marsh plants, but they grow quite well, though slowly, as underwater plants in soft, slightly acid water. The small and medium-sized species are regular inhabitants of almost every community tank and are in many ways ideal foreground plants.

Because of their slow growth, however, they are not very efficient in absorbing nutrient or as oxygenators in the aquarium.

Echinodorus

America. Underwater and marsh plants, some of which have become very widespread, particularly the large and small Amazon sword plants. They need plenty of light and nutrient, but grow quickly and therefore play a more significant part in the waste-absorbing processes than the species of *Cryptocoryne*.

Elodea

In temperate and subtropical regions of America and Europe. The tropical species are excellent, especially for the beginner's tank and the breeding tank. They grow rapidly and in bright conditions give off much oxygen. They will grow rooted in the gravel or floating. The genus *Lagarosiphon* is closely related.

Ludwigia

America. Underwater and marsh plants which grow rapidly.

Myriophyllum

WATER MILFOIL

Cosmopolitan. Several fast-growing species which have excellent decorative value in the community tank and are almost indispensable in the breeding tank. They will grow without being rooted but are best when planted in a group.

Sagittaria

ARROWHEAD

America and Europe. Underwater and marsh plants; most species have long, linear underwater leaves, whereas the emergent leaves have quite a different shape. Excellent, fast-growing plants.

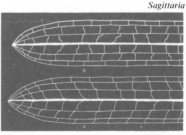

Sagittaria

Vallisneria

Vallisneria

Cosmopolitan. An underwater plant which is similar to *Sagittaria* but can be distinguished by the arrangement of the leaf veins. Excellent plants for the background and sides of a community tank. They increase extremely rapidly by means of runners.

ALGAE

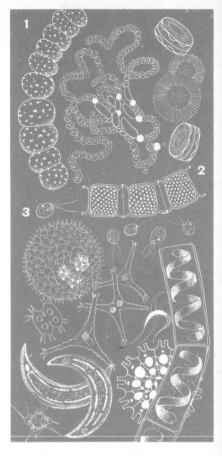

1. *blue-green algae, x ca. 700*
2. *diatoms, x c.a. 700*
3. *green algae, x ca. 50–700*

All the plants mentioned so far have belonged to the flowering plants or the ferns, which are the more advanced groups of the plant kingdom. The aquarist, however, also encounters the more primitive algae, a few as true aquarium plants and many as unwelcome guests.

Blue-green algae

Blue-green algae are not always harmful in themselves, but they are not very decorative and their presence indicates that there is something wrong with the biological balance, i.e. the content of waste or nutrient matter is much too high. Some kinds form an unattractive coating on aquarium plants.

One can rid the aquarium of them by the introduction of fast-growing plants, and particularly by reducing the light.

Diatoms

Occur as a brownish layer in poorly illuminated tanks, or in dark corners of well-illuminated ones. Diatoms have cell walls which contain silicic acid, which makes them very difficult to scrape off. They can be discouraged by improving the lighting in the aquarium, but they do not really do any damage.

Green algae and stoneworts

Two plants have won a permanent place in the aquarium: the green alga *Caulerpa prolifera* (page 159) in the marine tank and the stonewort *Nitella* (page 51) in freshwater tanks, particularly in those used for breeding.

Filamentous green algae

There are many species of varying length and thickness. They adhere very readily to plants and are thus easily introduced with new plants. They may be extremely troublesome as they form dense cushions covering the plants. Although they may be excellent in a breeding tank where they provide a refuge for eggs and fry, they are seldom welcome in the community tank. They can be kept in check by making a habit of rolling them on to a rough stick, but it is very difficult to remove them completely, as they have the same basic requirements as the decorative plants, so one cannot make conditions unfavourable for them without endangering the other plants as well. However, they do not survive very well in soft, slightly acid water, in which the nutrients are kept down by fast-growing plants.

Other green algae have quite short filaments and form fuzzy coverings on leaves. stones and glass. These species are, however, often consumed by plant-eating fishes and provided they do not actually cover the front glass, which must always be kept clean, they have a certain decorative value, especially on rocks and roots.

Free-floating green algae

These are microscopic green algae which sometimes make the aquarium water quite opaque and can be a great nuisance in a newly furnished tank. However, these suspended green algae are seldom a problem in a well-established tank. Protection from actual sunlight is often sufficient to stop an attack of 'green water'. These algae are also eaten by *Daphnia*, but if these crustaceans are used for control the fish must be removed for a time.

In general, a dense growth of algae, irrespective of the type, is an indication that something is wrong with the conditions in the tank.

VISITORS

In addition to the aquarium inhabitants proper – the fishes and plants – most tanks house a certain number of 'visitors', which may or may not be welcome.

SNAILS

Snails are among the best-established of these aquarium guests. At one time they were considered an essential part of every aquarium, but nowadays they are often unpopular and many aquarists will not have them. There is still some controversy about the role they play in the biological cycle. It is true that they consume a considerable amount of uneaten food and other organic material and thus help to speed up its breakdown. They do not, however, assist in cleansing the water, since what they consume is simply converted into small faeces and when they eventually die they merely add to the general pollution of the aquarium. Their role as glass cleaners is very limited. They certainly eat green algae as they creep across the glass but they by no means keep the panes clean. They do more good on leaves, which may be kept free of detritus by the activity of snails. They ordinarily do no actual damage to the plants, for they only eat leaves which are beginning to wither, not the young fresh ones, so whether one wishes to keep snails or not must be a matter of taste. However, it is best to avoid having large numbers of snails in a tank.

Incidentally, it is not always possible to control the situation, because snails' eggs can very easily be introduced on the leaves of plants, and once a snail population has become established in a tank it is almost impossible to wipe out. However, they do not thrive in soft, slightly acid water, and in such water the population will gradually die out.

The following species are frequently seen in aquaria.

Helisoma nigricans

RED RAMSHORN SNAIL

A rather small ramshorn with an exceptionally attractive red colour. This snail can be recommended if one really wants to have snails.

Ampullaria cuprina

A very large and peculiar snail which can reach a diameter of 2 in. In spite of its size it does not eat plants, but one must be wary of dead specimens of this species as a single one can pollute all the water in a small aquarium. The eggs are deposited on the surface of the water in large, hard, pinkish clusters. Known in the trade as the mystery snail.

Thiara (Melanoides) tuberculata

MALAYAN MUD SNAIL

An attractive species shaped like a tall spire. During the day it remains buried in the bottom and at night it can be found on the glass. Its habit of burrowing in the bottom is beneficial to the growth of the plants, but it may increase in numbers to such an extent as to become a nuisance.

Native European or North American snails should under no circumstances be used as they often house the fluke *Proalaria* (page 199).

OTHER VISITORS

Fish lice

The fish louse is a crustacean up to $\frac{1}{2}$ in. across, which is sometimes introduced into aquaria with live food. It clings to the skin of the fishes which it pierces to feed, and because of its large size it may kill them. The best method of control is to pick the lice off with a pair of forceps.

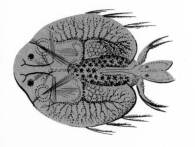

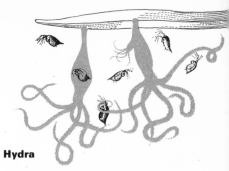

Hydra

The freshwater polyp *Hydra* is often brought in with live food. It does not harm adult fishes, and is in fact an interesting animal to have in an aquarium. Young fishes may, however, be caught by the tentacles of *Hydra*, and so may *Daphnia*. The easiest way of ridding the tank of them is to add copper, e.g. by hanging a couple of copper coins in the aquarium. As soon as the *Hydra* have disappeared the copper must be removed and half the water changed, because copper is also harmful to fishes. *Hydra* can also be killed by heating the tank water to 140°F, after first removing the fish.

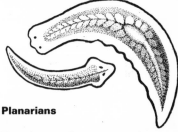

Planarians

Planarians or flatworms are also introduced with live food. They are even more harmless than *Hydra* but may attack fish eggs. Certain fishes, such as gouramis, paradise fish and *Pelmatochromis kribensis* eat planarians when they are hungry, but this is hardly an effective method of extermination. They can be killed by gradually heating the water to a temperature of about 95°F, but first remove the fishes and be careful of the aquarium plants.

DISEASES

Fishes are just as prone to disease as other living organisms, whether it is caused by poisoning, malnutrition, by virus or bacterial infections or by microscopic or macroscopic parasites.

Of the many hundreds of known fish diseases, several affect aquarium fishes, but a description of all these would be of little interest to the aquarist. In this section the most common illnesses are discussed with the emphasis laid on the aquarist's chance of making a diagnosis with simple means and of treating the condition successfully.

It is often claimed that the present-day rapid methods of transport, with fishes being moved from the place of collection to the aquarist in a couple of days, will mean healthier fishes than those formerly imported by slower methods of transport, which was usually by ship. This is incorrect, because with sea transport all the diseased fishes died on the way and only the healthiest survived the voyage, which actually provided an exceedingly effective and unavoidable period of quarantine. Nowadays, large numbers of fishes are put on the market only a few days after having been caught, or after having been kept in infected tanks by collectors and middlemen in the tropics and by importers. Most shopkeepers prefer to sell their fish immediately, before the diseases break out, rather than allow them to go through a costly, tiresome period of quarantine or risk having to treat the diseases themselves. After having bought aquarium fishes for some years, it is the author's opinion that almost a hundred per cent of the fishes bought from certain retailers and importers are infected with white spot. This cannot be seen on the shopkeeper's fishes, but it breaks out when the aquarist has installed them in his tank, that is, if he has not put them into strict quarantine first. However, many conscientious importers and dealers do quarantine their fishes. The aquarist would do well to seek out such dealers.

QUARANTINE

All newly bought fishes should be quarantined in a separate tank for about two weeks; this is the aquarist's most important rule.

But how does one find out whether a fish is healthy or not? This is not a problem for those who have even a minimum of experience in the aquarium hobby. Apart from the symptoms mentioned later in this section, a sick fish almost always behaves differently than a healthy one. It loses its appetite and often its colours, swims in a different way, often jerkily with the tail drooping (but bear in mind that many coralfishes normally have this jerky method of swimming) and sometimes hangs motionless below the surface of the water. Fishes that persistently have their dorsal fin folded down are likely to be sick.

Even a sick fish becomes lively when you want to catch it, but do not let this deceive you. Catch it and isolate it in a special tank so that it can be observed.

Poisoning

Aquarium fishes are forced to live in the water we give them; they cannot leave it and seek other places as in nature. As the water also comes into very intimate contact with the tissues of the fish – through the gills – every fluctuation in the composition of the water will affect the fish, and a change from the natural one is often harmful. Marked symptoms of poisoning are seldom observed in fishes, but one usually notices the general symptoms of sickness previously mentioned, and if the poisoning is not stopped the fish will die.

There are, in fact, no clear symptoms that indicate different types of poisoning. In each individual case the cause must be detected and removed.

Metals

Many metals and metallic salts are very poisonous even in small concentrations, especially in salt water where they are quickly dissolved, but also in fresh water. This is particularly true of copper and zinc. Certain cheap types of charcoal contain water-soluble zinc compounds which are poisonous; one must therefore always wash filter charcoal thoroughly before use, or avoid using charcoal altogether.

Chlorine

In many parts of the world, chlorine is added to drinking water, sometimes in quantities that are dangerous for fishes. In aquarium water and in tap water chlorine becomes bound as the compound chloramine, which cannot be eliminated by aeration. The best way to eliminate chloramine is to filter the water through activated charcoal.

Overfeeding and overcrowding

When there are too many fishes in the water or too much food, the decomposition of the food, which takes place with the aid of bacteria that require oxygen, causes a sharp drop in the oxygen content and often a decrease in the pH of the water, i.e. it becomes more acid. If these changes occur suddenly they can affect the fishes, especially marine fishes; in any case, their resistance to disease is lowered so that they are more easily infected with *Oodinium* and fish tuberculosis. The cure is obviously fewer fishes and sparser feeding. A less satisfactory solution is to filter the water more thoroughly and to change it more often.

Ichthyophthirius multifiliis

WHITE SPOT OR ITCH

No disease is more feared by aquarists. This is because it is by far the most widespread of the serious fish diseases, and if it is not treated it can wipe out a whole stock of fish. The disease is recognized by the presence of large white, granular spots, $\frac{1}{2}$–1 mm. across, on the body and fins, almost as though fine salt had been shaken onto the fish. These patches itch, and one can see the fish rub itself against plants to relieve the irritation. The fish may only have one patch, and this may disappear in a few days – but don't let this deceive you. The patch has fallen off and divided itself, and in a week's time all the fishes in the aquarium may be covered with white spots. If they survive this attack, a third, much worse attack will break out in another week and this will probably kill all the fishes or weaken them so much that they succumb to other diseases.

This parasite is a unicellular protozoan animal which lies under the outer skin layer of the fish. Under the microscope the cell is seen to contain a darker, horseshoe-shaped nucleus, and the whole animal can be seen to turn round with the help of a covering of cilia. This rotating movement is characteristic of *Ichthyophthirius* in contrast to *Oodinium*. After some time on the skin or gills of the fish, the parasite bores its way out, falls to the bottom and divides into many tiny individuals which immediately swim around in search of new host fishes. If they do not find a fish in a few days they will die. It is extremely difficult to attack the parasite when it is embedded in the tissues of the fish, but it is very vulnerable when swimming freely. White spot can be treated by adding a drug to the water which kills the free-swimming young. Many such drugs are available on the market, and several of these are effective, but it is important that one keeps to the prescribed length of treatment. Effective treatment is more rapid if the temperature is raised to about 90°F.

Most of these drugs are injurious to plants, so the treatment must be carried out in a separate tank without vegetation. If the original tank with its plants is allowed to stand without fish for a few days the remaining *Ichthyophthirius* spores will die and the healthy fishes can then be put back without risk. But be sure that no fishes are left behind during the cure, even if they are apparently healthy because they may house several tiny parasites, so that the disease can start afresh.

Sometimes *Ichthyophthirius* subsides with no outside help and one may see no more of it. It often breaks out again, however, if a new fish is put into the tank, even if this fish is apparently healthy. Also, the susceptibility of different fishes to this disease differs considerably. White spot is essentially a freshwater disease and the commonly occurring type of parasite cannot survive in salt water. Fishes that can tolerate this type of water can be cured by being kept for some time in brackish or salt water.

There is, however, a so-called salt water *Ichthyophthirius* which produces the same symptoms as the freshwater form, but it is not usually lethal. The life cycle of the parasite is shorter and the normal drugs used against the freshwater form do not appear to be effective.

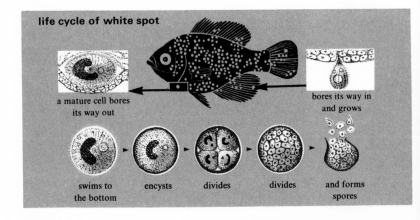

life cycle of white spot

a mature cell bores its way out

bores its way in and grows

swims to the bottom   encysts   divides   divides   and forms spores

Oodinium

In freshwater fishes, an *Oodinium* infection is often referred to as a 'cold' because it becomes apparent if the fishes have been subjected to a fall in temperature. In some respects the symptoms resemble those produced by *Ichthyophthirius*, but the white spots are usually much smaller so that the fish looks as though it is covered with fine powder. Seen through the microscope the spots are seen as individual parasites (dinoflagellates), which are motionless and have a round nucleus. *Oodinium* is probably present in most aquaria and one cannot count on exterminating it. It attacks primarily cyprinids, toothcarps and labyrinth fishes and, as previously mentioned, usually occurs in conjunction with other debilities. To prevent its occurrence one should avoid sudden drops in temperature.

The *Oodinium* that attacks marine fishes is presumably a different flagellate, but it causes the same symptoms – a light powdery layer which particularly attacks the eyes and its outbreaks are associated with other debilities. It can be cured with copper sulphate; 1 g. of copper sulphate is dissolved in a quart of distilled water and 1 ml. of this solution is used for every 2 quarts of aquarium water. Charcoal filters should be stopped, but other filtration can continue. It is not necessary to change the water, as the copper is deposited as an insoluble non-poisonous compound.

Ichthyophonus

Ichthyophonus disease is extremely widespread, but difficult to diagnose and impossible to cure. It is caused by spherical phycomycetes, $5-20\,\mu$ across, which attack the internal organs, where they accumulate as tiny brown to black spheres. The fishes

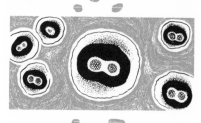

infect each other either from open sores or abscesses or by eating infected dead fishes. The symptoms can be very varied: hollow belly, sores, abscesses, bulging eyes, lop-

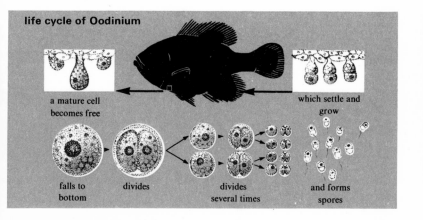

life cycle of Oodinium

a mature cell becomes free

which settle and grow

falls to bottom   divides   divides several times   and forms spores

sided body, etc. The disease is by no means always lethal. It is impossible to cure, but one can reduce the possibility of infection by immediately removing all fish which show signs of the disease.

Fish tuberculosis

Fish tuberculosis is very widespread among aquarium fishes, especially the older domesticated forms, such as guppies, mollies and Siamese fighting fish. Like the type of tuberculosis which attacks warm-blooded animals, it is caused by rod-shaped bacteria, and the disease breaks out particularly when the fish is in a weakened condition, e.g. in late autumn when the food has less nutritional value. The symptoms are slower movements and disturbance of balance, and an examination of the gills will show well-defined fiery red patches. Deaths due to this parasite are common, especially in densely populated aquaria. To prevent it one must remove any fishes that show signs of sickness and give the remainder as varied a diet as possible, perhaps with the addition of a vitamin preparation.

It is not normally possible to cure fish tuberculosis, although in several cases considerable improvement has been observed after the addition of sphagnum moss. Fish tuberculosis *cannot* infect human beings or other warm-blooded animals.

Neon disease

Caused by *Plistophora hyphessobryconis,* which primarily attacks neon tetras and other characins, but other groups can be infected. The fishes swim about restlessly and lack appetite, and in the neon tetra there may be characteristic discoloration. The spores often settle on the fins so that

when the fishes nip each other the spores are transferred from one to the other.

It is hardly possible to cure this disease,

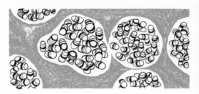

but it can be combated to a certain extent by keeping the fishes for a fortnight in a solution of euflavin and methylene blue.

Raising of the scales or dropsy

Sometimes a fish appears to be blown up, so that the scales are raised, giving the body the appearance of a pine-cone. This is caused by dropsy, an accumulation of liquid in the body, and is not really a disease in itself, but a symptom of several. Fish suffering from dropsy should be killed straight away or isolated, as they cannot be cured.

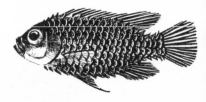

Bulging eyes

Bulging eyes are sometimes seen in freshwater and especially in marine fishes. This is a symptom of several diseases and the condition may subside of its own accord, but sometimes it is necessary to kill the fish.

Worm cataract

This condition, which blinds the affected fish, is caused by a parasitic fluke, *Proalaria* or *Diplostomum*, which has three intermediate hosts. One of these is a bird, and when the eggs of the parasite fall into the water with the bird's droppings, they hatch into a stage which enters a freshwater snail. This stage develops into fork-tailed cercariae which spread out in the water and attack the fish. One should never, therefore, put newly caught freshwater snails into the aquarium. There is no cure for this disease.

Fungal infections

Wounds on fishes are often attacked by fungus, which appears as a layer looking like a mould. This may spread to the musculature of the fish, thus causing its death. A euflavin bath is normally sufficient to cure this disease (1 g. euflavin to 100 l. water). Aureomycin, 13 mg. to a quart of water is more effective, but a prescription is necessary to obtain it.

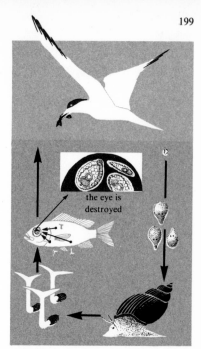

the eye is destroyed

Skilled aquarists frequently cure fungus by removing the sick fish in a net and carefully painting the affected area with mercurochrome.

THE FRESHWATER AQUARIUM

The preceding sections of this book have been concerned with the inhabitants of the aquarium – the fishes, plants and visitors. The following paragraphs deal with certain technical problems which face the aquarist.

There are many different types of aquarium, but they fall into two main groups: marine aquaria and freshwater aquaria. The types of water used and the different kinds of fish which can be kept in them are not the only factors which separate these two groups. There are great differences between the problems facing marine and freshwater aquarists and so the text has been divided into two sections, just as the freshwater and marine fishes were discussed separately in the systematic part of the book.

TECHNICAL AIDS

The numerous technical aids available to the aquarist make it possible, with little effort and at low cost, to achieve the necessary conditions for the fishes in his aquarium. However, it should be a major rule for the less experienced aquarist (and also indeed for the more experienced) to manage with as few technical aids as possible. Many of these are often superfluous and they may go wrong, with fatal results. In a biologically well-balanced aquarium, that is a tank with the correct relationship between the numbers of fishes and plants, only artificial lighting is needed, and possibly a heater if the tank is kept in a cool place.

Lighting

Natural illumination is much too temperamental, being too strong in summer, too weak in winter, and absent during the evening when the aquarist wishes to enjoy his aquarium. So the tank should be equipped with artificial lighting, preferably in the form of an enclosed fitting which rests on top of the aquarium. These fittings can be bought ready-made or they can be home-made of wood or metal. Illumination is usually by fluorescent tubes, which provide excellent light at wavelengths that the aquarium plants can utilize. This is a cheap form of lighting, since there is little wastage in the form of heat rays. The plants prefer a cold, bluish light, but the so-called warm white or de luxe tubes, which emit a greater proportion of red rays are more attractive. The tubes can be combined with a bulb, perhaps a spotlight which can be switched on in the evening and this will give a more attractive effect in the tank than the rather cold, shadowless light from the fluorescent tubes. The aquarium lighting should be switched on for about twelve hours daily. At present, many aquarists favour fluorescent tubes of the Grolux type which send out an excess of red and blue rays. This type of tube encourages plant growth and emphasizes the red and blue colours, particularly of iridescent fishes such as the neon tetras. Many, however, think that this type of lighting gives the aquarium a garish, artificial appearance.

Heating

In a room where the temperature is kept constant at a temperature of 70°F or higher the aquarium needs no further source of heating than the small amount given out by the light fitting. If the water temperature remains at 71–75°F during the day and 64–68°F at night, this is sufficient for most fishes. It does not matter that the surface temperature is considerably higher than the bottom temperature, due to the lighting system; this is comparable to conditions in natural standing waters.

A number of fishes, however, particularly the labyrinth fishes, prefer a temperature of 75–82°F, and for these one must provide extra heating. Electric heaters, which are now universal, are usually rod-shaped and can be hidden in a corner or on the bottom near the rear wall. These heaters should normally be used in conjunction with a thermostat, of which small, durable and reliable aquarium versions are readily available. The best heaters have a thermostat in the heating tube.

Aeration

Aeration is not absolutely necessary in a normally populated tank. The water is oxygenated sufficiently from the surface and by the activity of the plants. The primary function of aeration is to stir the water; this increases the absorption of oxygen at the surface, and keeps the temperature evenly distributed. If there are so many fishes that aeration is neces-sary, one must normally also filter the water, and the aeration is used to drive the filter.

Filtration

An overcrowded aquarium, a breeding tank or an aquarium with fishes that dig and disturb the substrate can be very difficult to keep clean, and in such cases a filter must be used. Basically, this consists of a waterproof box which is packed with various substances through which the water flows. Filters are available in all shapes and sizes, and they are designed either to be put into the tank (internal filter) or to hang outside it (external filter). A filter inside the aquarium is less obvious, but its capacity is often small, and it may be difficult to change the filtration medium. If filtration is only required spasmodically, an external filter is to be recommended. The water is drawn through the filter by a water or air pump. The air pump is preferable since this oxygenates the water at the same time.

The materials in the filter are very varied; sand and gravel are often used in

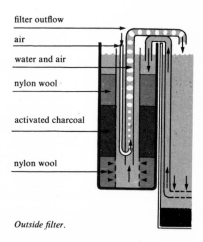

filter outflow

air

water and air

nylon wool

activated charcoal

nylon wool

Outside filter.

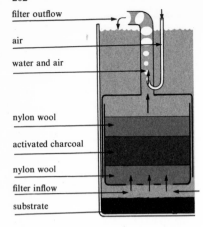

filter outflow

air

water and air

nylon wool

activated charcoal

nylon wool

filter inflow

substrate

filters consist quite simply of a foam-rubber sponge through which the water is drawn. This sponge can be removed and washed thoroughly under the tap and is an excellent filter for the small aquarium.

A bottom filter can even be recommended for an aquarium in biological equilibrium. This is a shallow box which is placed beneath the substrate in the tank. With the help of a current of air, the water is drawn down through the substrate into the box and thence through a tube back into the water. The substrate acts as a filter medium which traps the impurities.

large filters, but in smaller filters nylon wool or fibreglass is excellent since it removes green algae and the turbidity caused by overfeeding. Activated charcoal absorbs colouring matter and some of the breakdown products of the fishes, but it has only a limited capacity. It must be changed very regularly and should always be used in conjunction with another material, e.g. nylon wool which will trap the larger waste particles. Some internal

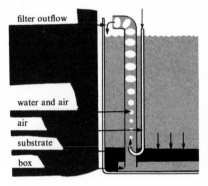

filter outflow

water and air

air

substrate

box

THE WATER

In nature most aquarium fishes live in soft, slightly acid water, whereas in the aquarium they often have to live in hard, slightly alkaline water, since the underground strata from which most of our water is obtained is radically different from that of the tropics. This creates problems in the case of a great number of fishes, but these can usually be surmounted. One does not necessarily need to have an exhaustive knowledge of the chemistry of water in order to enjoy the aquarium hobby, and if one finds this aspect of it boring, it is probably best to skip the subject altogether rather than labour with it. In fact, most fishes are so tolerant that they thrive even under quite unnatural conditions, although many will find it difficult to breed under such conditions.

Hardness

In nature no water is absolutely chemically pure, as it always contains various substances in solution. In northern Europe and North America, salts of the element calcium, such as calcium carbonate or calcium sulphate, are permanent constituents of all natural waters as well as of piped water. Water with a high calcium and/or magnesium content is known as hard water, water with a low calcium and magnesium content as soft water. Many fishes are very tolerant of the hardness of the water, others are extremely sensitive to it, e.g. many species from the rain-forests.

The aquarist often needs to measure the hardness of the water. At one time various complicated methods were used, but a special measuring kit is now available, consisting of an indicator and tablets which have to be dissolved in the water.

pH (acidity)

Many of the substances that are dissolved in the water affect the acidity of the water so that it does not react in an absolutely neutral way as chemically pure water would. One of these substances is the dissolved calcium and hard water tends to be alkaline. The pH value is given in numbers; a value of 7 represents neutral water, while higher numbers mean that the water becomes increasingly alkaline, and lower numbers that it becomes more and more acid. Hard water almost always has a pH between 7 and 8, whereas soft rain-forest water often has a pH between 6 and 7. The pH value can be measured with various indicators which are available on the market. Indicator paper is cheap but not accurate and indicator solutions are best. For aquarium use these solutions must have a pH range from 5 to 8. If one measures the pH of the aquarium frequently, one can see that it fluctuates over a period of 24 hours; this is because the pH is affected by the amount of carbon dioxide dissolved in the water. In an aquarium with plants but no aeration the pH is therefore lowest at night and highest during the daytime.

Adjusting the pH

No attempt should be made to change the pH of hard water. In soft water the pH can be lowered by very carefully adding a weak solution of phosphoric acid. In exceptional circumstances it is possible to raise the pH by adding small amounts of washing soda. Ordinarily, attempting to adjust the pH and hardness of water is not worth the trouble.

The choice of aquarium water

The aquarist should choose between the following two types of water:

1. Hard, slightly alkaline water, which in most places means plain tap water. In districts where the tap water is very soft, small pieces of limestone or chalk can be placed in the tank, e.g. in the substrate or in the filter; these will eventually increase the hardness of the water and the pH will adjust to the desired value.

2. Soft, slightly acid water (rain-forest water). Here it is easiest to buy demineralized or distilled water, which should be aerated for a few days before it is used, and can possibly be mixed with tap water. If large quantities of soft water are needed, it is worth the aquarist removing the calcium himself by using a demineralizing filter. In an aquarium with soft water it is essential that the gravel and the decorative materials used do not contain calcium. These materials can be placed in hydrochloric acid for a time before use. Boiled, long-fibred sphagnum makes an excellent substrate; it tends to keep the pH constant at the required slightly acid value and it makes an exceptionally attractive and natural-looking substrate. To prevent the sphagnum colouring the water too much it can be first left in a strong soda solution; subsequent washing removes most of the dark colouring matter.

FURNISHING THE INTERIOR

For most freshwater aquarists the plants provide the main form of interior furnishing, provided that the fishes kept will tolerate plants. The method of planting used in most community tanks is not really natural, but it is attractive and enhances the appearance of one's underwater 'garden'. It consists of an open area for swimming near the front glass, behind which are low, dense groups of plants, e.g. *Cryptocoryne*, and further back some taller species which will cover both the side and rear walls. The gravel is lowest at the front of the tank and rises towards the back thus creating an impression of space. This kind of interior decoration can be improved by the addition of roots or branches, or rocks of a suitable size and colour. The rocks should always be placed as they appear in nature, resting on the largest surface. If they are placed on end, the aquarium will resemble a cemetery more than a rocky landscape. To provide a cave for fish that dig, it is best to use a large flat stone, supported by smaller ones. The supporting stones should rest directly on the bottom of the tank, otherwise the fishes will dig until the whole arrangement disappears into the gravel.

Individual taste should be allowed a free hand in setting up the interior decoration and very beautiful effects can often be obtained by breaking the rules.

In recent years a flood of artificial objects to put in the aquarium have appeared, especially from America; divers, treasure chests, wrecks, etc., or cottages designed to camouflage an aerator, where the bubbles are the "smoke" from the chimney. These objects usually produce a feeling of horror in the genuine aquarist, not only as a matter of taste but also because they introduce an incorrect sense of proportion into the aquarium. The aquarium is a piece of nature in its natural size. The introduction of incorrectly proportioned artificial objects makes the fishes look like giant flying monsters and ruins the very foundation of the aquarist's hobby, which is to bring a tiny portion of nature into his home.

1 *Anubias lanceolatum*
2 *Echinodorus tenellus*
3 *Aponogeton ulvaceus*
4 *Vallisneria spiralis*
5 *Cryptocoryne nevillii*
6 root
7 branch
8 rock

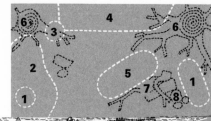

FOOD AND FEEDING

In nature most aquarium fishes feed on small live food which lives in the water or which falls down onto the surface; food is sometimes snapped up from the vegetation just above the surface. In addition, some fishes feed on live – or dead – organic matter on the bottom. Many fishes, especially the larger ones, graze algae and the finer leaves of the plants, partly for the vegetable matter itself, but mainly to utilize the numerous small animals to be found there.

In many tropical waters the natural food animals such as small free-swimming crustaceans – which the aquarist thinks of as live food – are very sparse. A considerable amount of the natural food of tropical fishes comes from the air, in the form of insects that fall onto the surface of the water. In nature most fishes are continuously searching for food, and they feed almost constantly. It is, therefore, difficult to accustom them to few, relatively large meals. As far as possible the aquarist should give several small meals. On the other hand, short, or even quite long periods without food will not harm the fishes. Well-fed aquarium fishes can comfortably survive for as long as two weeks or more without food. The golden rule is never to give the fishes more food than they can consume in a couple of minutes and dried food should be eaten before it reaches the bottom, unless the tank contains catfishes or other fishes which only take food from the bottom. Even *Daphnia* should be given in limited quantities, because many fishes, when they have had enough to eat, have the habit of snapping at these crustaceans and then spitting them out in a damaged condition. The *Daphnia* then fall to the bottom and die.

Dried food

Nowadays there are many suitable brands of dried food, usually rolled out into fine flakes. Well established brands of dried food are excellent and can be used as a basic diet for most fishes. The brands can be changed occasionally to provide variety. In addition one can give small amounts of cod roe, fish and any other scraps from the kitchen which are considered suitable, but spiced and fatty foods and any mammal flesh must be avoided.

Daphnia

Daphnia or water-fleas are a very valuable live food, if one can obtain them from a pond or from aquarium retailers. There are several species of *Daphnia*, distributed in all types of fresh water. These hard-shelled crustaceans are an excellent food which should be given regularly to aquarium fishes if a source of supply can be found. An appropriately balanced diet of *Daphnia* and dry food is ideal for most aquarium fishes.

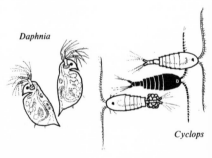

Daphnia

Cyclops

Cyclops

The species of *Cyclops* are considerably smaller crustaceans than *Daphnia*. They are both to be found in the same places, although often at different times of the year. *Cyclops* is not as good a food as *Daphnia*, and since it is a predator it should not be put into the breeding tank.

Mosquito and midge larvae

In Europe the transparent phantom larvae *(Corethra)* are sometimes available, especially in winter. In spite of their delicate appearance, these are an excellent and nutritious food which will live for a long time if kept cold. It does not matter if the larvae hatch out as the adult flies cannot bite.

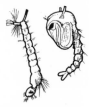

The black larvae of *Culex* and other genera are the young stages of the biting gnats or mosquitoes. They are to be found in the spring on or near the surface of the water and can be scooped off with a net. They make an excellent food, but they should be fed in small enough quantities to ensure that none live long enough to become adult.

Red midge larvae (chironomids) live in mud tubes at the bottom of pools, often in large quantities. They are also an exceptionally good food for fishes and they keep well.

Tubifex

These are small worms that live on the bottom in polluted waters. They can often be bought from aquarium dealers, especially in winter, and they live for a long time if kept in slow-flowing cold water. They are not a particularly good food, but can be used to provide some variety in the diet.

Whiteworms (enchytraeids)

Small worms, related to earthworms, which are cultured in boxes of soil where they are fed on oats or other cereals. They are a rather fattening food which should only be given in small quantities.

Fruitflies (Drosophila)

They can easily be cultured on rotting fruit (e.g. banana) or on a fermenting mixture of cornflakes and water. They are excellent food, but most aquarium fishes have to be gradually 'trained' to take them. Vestigial-winged varieties, which cannot fly, can be bought.

Frozen foods

Most of the live foods mentioned above, as well as adult and young brine shrimps *(Artemia)*, can be bought frozen from tropical fish stores. Frozen foods are nearly as nutritious as their living counterparts and they are much more convenient to use. Chunks of frozen food may be dropped into the water. As the food thaws, the fishes eagerly devour it.

BREEDING

It is often said that when so many of our animals breed in captivity it is a sign that they are thriving. Perhaps one should reverse this and say that if animals do not breed in captivity it is a sign that something is drastically wrong, since the urge to reproduce is fundamental to all animals.

Fortunately, a large number of freshwater aquarium fishes do breed, or at least make active attempts to do so. It is to be hoped that in time the marine aquarist will also learn to master his subject to the extent that sea-water fishes will also breed in captivity.

It would be impossible to give detailed instructions on how to breed aquarium fishes. Different species have widely different requirements; also, the reports one hears on how to breed difficult fishes often differ fundamentally.

The condition of the parents

The basis of breeding is a pair of healthy parents. This usually means adult, but not old, fishes that have been given as varied a diet as possible and are in prime condition. In nature, many fishes lay eggs regularly each season, or at regular intervals from the time they become sexually mature until they die. They need to spawn at regular intervals, otherwise the eggs become sterile. It is therefore most satisfactory to raise one's own breeding fishes and use them as soon as they are sexually mature.

Spawning

It is usually best, in the first place, to buy a number of young fish and allow them to pair off by themselves. In the livebearing species, fertilization – often accompanied by a complex courtship – usually takes place in the community tank and, for the safety of the young, the female should merely be isolated some time before giving birth. But many egg-laying species refuse to spawn in the community tank, or if they do the results are nil, because the other fishes eat all the eggs. One must therefore set up a special breeding aquarium. It is an advantage to put the male and female into the breeding tank at intervals of a few days, for the enforced separation often induces mating. In many species the breeding process can be initiated by the addition of fresh water, comparable to the beginning of the rainy season in nature, and some fishes mate at certain times of day, e.g. when the morning sun shines on the tank, or when it gets dark in the evening. Most rain-forest fishes require soft, slightly acid water in the breeding tank, even if they are normally kept in hard water. If the fish eat the eggs, the aquarium should be planted with fine-leaved vegetation or the bottom can be covered with small stones or marbles, between which the eggs will be hidden. Alternatively one can install a fine-mesh grating an inch above the bottom. If the fishes practice brood protection, like many cichlids, the pairs should obviously remain, but otherwise the fish are put back into the community tank after spawning.

Feeding the young

The newly hatched young usually have a yolk sac which contains sufficient nourishment for a few days, often a week, and during this time they should not be fed. This is followed by a difficult period in the rearing of the young, which should always have full stomachs and be given as varied a diet as possible. Fine dried food is only taken by a few large fry and the rearing of the young should not be based on this. Finely mashed hard-boiled egg yolk can be given to many young fishes, but this is not sufficient either.

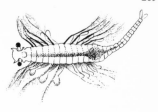

BRINE SHRIMP

Dried eggs of the brine shrimp *(Artemia salina)* can be bought. These eggs are put into a jar of salt water (20 g. cooking salt to one litre at 77°F). After 1–2 days they hatch and the tiny nauplii which collect on the light side of the jar can be sucked out with a pipette. An excellent food, easily obtained and easily prepared.

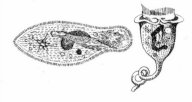

INFUSORIANS

A culture of infusorians (semi-microscopic protozoan animals) can be started by putting banana peel, hay and a few drops of milk in a jar of water and leaving it for a week. The banana peel and hay are then removed and the culture is fed every other day with a few drops of milk. Swarms of infusorians develop and one can pour some of this culture into the aquarium and then fill up the stock culture with tap water. A purer sample of infusorians can be obtained by pouring the culture water into a bottle and plugging the neck with a wad of cotton-wool inserted a few centimetres below the surface of the water. As the amount of oxygen in the bottle decreases the infusorians work their way up through the cotton-wool and can then be drawn off with the upper few centimetres of water. These infusorians, consisting mainly of species of *Paramecium*, form an excellent starting food for very young fishes.

PLANKTON

The most varied and therefore the best food for young fishes is plankton, which can be collected in the wild with the help of a special fine-mesh plankton net. Relatively large planktonic animals, mainly *Cyclops*, must be sieved off as they may attack the fry.

As the young fish develop it may be necessary to sort them according to size or the smallest will not get enough to eat.

THE MARINE AQUARIUM

Marine fishes are much more difficult to keep than freshwater fishes. One should not attempt to keep them merely because one is attracted by the beauty of the coral-fishes. On the other hand, the difficulties can be overcome. The numbers of marine aquarists are steadily increasing and those who take their hobby seriously derive great pleasure from it and find that their fishes thrive and show even greater activity than many freshwater fishes. The first results of breeding successes in the marine aquarium are now appearing.

THE TANK

Salt water dissolves metals and the resulting substances are generally poisonous to fishes. Pure iron, which is almost non-poisonous, is an exception, but iron is so fiercely attacked by sea water that it rapidly rusts away. Copper and zinc compounds are extremely dangerous and even most types of stainless steel are affected. This means that all types of metal are taboo in the marine aquarium, including, of course, any metal in the pumps and other objects which may come into contact with the water. As a result of this corrosive action, one can only choose the ordinary frame type of aquarium tank after careful consideration and it must be thoroughly coated before use. This can be done by covering the scrupulously clean frame with a two-component plastic skin (epoxy resin) of the same type as that used for coating fibreglass boats.

Enamelled frames are beginning to appear on the market, and these are excellent, provided the enamel is un-damaged. Plastic frames are also obtainable, but these are often so delicate that the tank soon leaks. Plastic or glass tanks that are glued together are frequently used, but glued glass tanks tend to come apart at the joints.

The glass must be fixed to the frame with a cement that has been specially prepared for use in sea water since ordinary aquarium cement may be attacked by the water and some cements are toxic to marine fishes.

Aquaria manufactured especially for marine use are available. Anyone beginning with marine fishes would be well advised to buy one.

THE WATER

In most cases the freshwater aquarist can simply draw his water from the tap, but conditions are far more complicated for the marine aquarist. If he lives near the sea, and the salinity is sufficiently high, he can use natural sea water, but the use of artificial salt water is becoming more and more common. Formulae are now available so that the aquarist can prepare artificial sea water from tap water. Salt from a recognized manufacturer, used according to the directions, gives salt water that is as good as or even better than sea water, even for the most delicate organisms.

Salinity

Aquarists who keep marine invertebrates usually use water with a salinity close to that of the oceans, namely 3·5 per cent (specific gravity 1·025). If only fishes are kept, it is often possible to lower the salinity to 2·5–3 per cent (1·018). When the nitrate content of the water is high (from accumulated waste products) a lower salinity appears to protect the fishes against the attacks of the parasitic dino-flagellate, *Oodinium*. The more saline the water, the heavier it is, and one can therefore measure the percentage of salt by using a small hydrometer, which indicates the specific gravity. At 77°F a salinity of 3·5 per cent is equivalent to a specific gravity of 1·025, while 2·5 per cent is equivalent to a specific gravity of 1·018. A hydrometer calibrated for the specific gravity of water is an essential tool of the marine aquarist.

Care of the water

In nature where the ratio of water volume to the number of fishes is enormous, the salt water of the oceans constitutes an extremely stable medium. In the aquarium we have a large number of fishes in a small volume of water, and each day add nutrient in the form of fish food. Whether this is consumed by the fishes and subsequently excreted, or whether it falls to the bottom, it contributes to an accumulation of nitrogenous metabolic products in the water. These substances are broken down from ammonia to nitrite and nitrate, a process of decomposition which takes place with the help of bacteria and which requires oxygen. Ammonia and some of the other intermediates are extremely poisonous, and it is therefore imperative that they are broken down further – to nitrate – as quickly as possible.

This is mainly done in the filter, where the through flow of water provides the basis for an enormous production of bacteria. Ammonia is broken down more quickly when this aggregation of bacteria is large; so the filter must not be cleaned too often. The end product of the process, nitrate, is by no means so poisonous as ammonia, but as it is the end product, it accumulates. Many invertebrates are affected by even small quantities of nitrates, but most fishes tolerate 500–600 mg. per

litre, and a few robust fishes can stand up to 1000 mg. per litre. Since the nitrate cannot be extracted from the water, the only way in which the increasing nitrate content can be reduced is by periodically changing part of the water. The amount to be removed at a time depends on how delicate the aquarium animals are, how economically one feeds them and on whether there is a flourishing growth of algae which can be harvested, for algae use and remove a certain amount of nitrogen. A change of about a third of the aquarium water every other month is normally sufficient.

Foam filter or protein skimmers

In the foam filter or protein skimmers used by some marine aquarists, air and water are mixed in a chamber. The proteins and their immediate breakdown products, but not nitrite and nitrate, then become bound to the surface of the bubbles and the stiff foam that works its way up out of the foam filter is much richer in nitrogen than the water in the tank. The

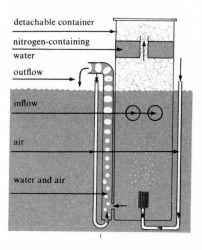

detachable container

nitrogen-containing water

outflow

inflow

air

water and air

foam is discarded and in this way the foam filter delays – but does not prevent – the build up of a high nitrate content.

Ozone

Ozone is often added to the air in a foam filter. Ozone is a form of oxygen in which three oxygen atoms are linked, one of them very loosely. This atom can therefore easily leave the molecule and link up with other substances which thus become oxidized. The efficiency of the foam filter is greatly increased when ozone is used in it.

Ozone aeration without the use of a foam filter causes the more rapid oxidation of food remains and the like, so that the water becomes clearer and the greasy bacterial layer, which sometimes appears on the surface, disappears. It is debatable whether such ozone aeration has any positive value apart from an aesthetic one; the breakdown process occurs anyway and the crystal clear water may give the aquarist a sense of false security. Ozone is very poisonous to the fishes and it can therefore only be used in a separate chamber through which the water flows.

Ultraviolet light

Ultraviolet irradiation, which kills bacteria, is sometimes used. It is not really possible to sterilize the aquarium water completely; indeed this would scarcely be desirable, but the number of bacteria can be considerably reduced. Whether it is, in fact, an advantage to reduce the number of bacteria is still uncertain.

pH

The marine aquarist has to be much more aware of the acidity of the water than the freshwater aquarist. The acidity in a marine tank fluctuates more readily and

such fluctuations are less tolerated. The pH should lie between 8·2 and 8·4 and excessive feeding or a filter that is too dirty can easily cause the pH to drop. When the cause of the drop has been remedied, the pH can be carefully raised again by the addition of sodium bicarbonate. Ample quantities of limestone, chalk or coral, e.g. as part of the decoration, are to be recommended, as these substances produce an excellent buffer effect. There is a special pH indicator on the market for measuring the acidity of salt water.

FOOD

Marine fishes are generally easy to feed. Most species quickly become accustomed to dead food though not normally to dried food. Raw or boiled, chopped mussel, shrimp, lean fish or fish roe are excellent foods, but remember that feeding should be limited.

Daphnia and mosquito larvae are taken by many fishes, but as they only survive a few minutes in salt water one must be careful only to give as much as will be eaten immediately. A better type of live food is newly-hatched, or slightly older brine shrimp *(Artemia)*, a crustacean whose eggs can withstand desiccation and are therefore sold all over the world. The eggs hatch in salt water with slight aeration. If the aquarist lives near the sea or brackish water he can catch animals for food just as one can in fresh water, and when attempting to breed marine fishes, it is probably rather important to feed the fry on plankton from the sea.

Another suitable animal food, which can be caught in large numbers at certain times of the year, is the crustacean *Mysis*. It can, if necessary, be frozen for later use.

Some fishes need a vegetable diet, among others, the surgeon-fishes, which require algae or chopped spinach. Certain marine fishes are 'food specialists', e.g. many of the Plectognathi (boxfishes and

pufferfishes) feed on snails, bivalves and crustaceans, but they will eat other food. Sea-horses need live food of a certain size, such as *Mysis*, brine shrimp or newborn guppies.

DISEASE

The disease most often encountered by the marine aquarist is *Oodinium,* which breaks out as soon as any weakness occurs. This and the salt-water *Ichthyophthirius* are discussed on page 197.

GROUPING THE FISHES

Fresh water aquarists are usually advised to keep fishes in schools. Unfortunately,

the marine aquarist can rarely do this. The fishes he keeps are primarily coral-fishes, and these are almost all territorial, each individual having its own area which is vigorously defended against its fellows, whereas fishes of other species are tolerated. Sometimes male and female share a territory, but it is more usual for each individual to have its own, and since even the smallest territory is larger than a private tank of normal size, only one specimen of each species can be kept. On the other hand, several species can generally be kept together. Young fishes usually get on well together but as soon as they begin to reach sexual maturity they become quarrelsome and, if one is not aware of the problem, the weaker fishes may be mutilated or killed. Also, there may only be a limited number of hiding-places in the tank, so that a newly-arrived fish cannot find an unoccupied place of refuge. It may, therefore, be an advantage to rearrange the corals in the tank when new fishes are introduced, so that all the occupants of the aquarium are busy finding new hiding places and do not have time to attack the newcomers.

REMEMBER TO QUARANTINE
all new fish

INTERIOR DECORATION

With a few exceptions, plants will not grow in marine tanks. One of the exceptions is the Mediterranean alga *Caulerpa prolifera* (illustrated on page 159) which may grow into attractive clumps. The marine aquarist is usually obliged to decorate with dead material, and naturally, corals are most frequently used. Living colonies of corals are usually brown or green, but most dead corals stems are white. Many prefer, therefore, to stain them in natural-looking colours. The well-cleaned and dried corals can be stained with alcohol-soluble aniline dyes which can be sprayed on. After drying for a few days, the corals are then finished with a durable varnish. The best results are obtained with a polymerizing two-component epoxy resin. The coral is coated twice with this substance, with an interval of a few days; this is best done by shaking the coral around in a plastic bag filled with the resin.

The background must not detract from the beauty of the fishes; so it is best to keep the colours as muted as possible. The usual method of arranging the corals is to use the same basic principles as when furnishing a freshwater tank, e.g. the lowest corals in front, building up in height towards the back. Of course one can do this, but it often looks unnatural and a more pleasing effect can be obtained by using a more natural arrangement.

In nature large blocks of coral rise out of the level sand-covered sea bed and there may be overhangs, bridges, etc. The marine aquarist can simulate this by mounting his corals on slabs of limestone or cement which lines the side walls of the tank, and extend up to the surface. The bottom of the aquarium can be covered with loose sand, with perhaps a single low coral. The back wall can also be decorated in the same way. Alternatively an illusion of great depth can be created by fitting a semi-transparent sheet behind the rear glass and placing some dry corals even further back. A tank furnished in this way will contrast with the interior of the usual freshwater tank. The fishes will also have more free swimming space, and uneaten food can easily be removed from the bottom.

If one keeps fishes from the Mediterranean Sea or from the rocky coasts of the tropics, corals are, of course, not appropriate. For these, the tank can be decorated purely with rocks, but here again there must be plenty of hiding-places, which should not be too deep or inaccessible; otherwise the removal of a dead fish or food remains will be impossible.

BIBLIOGRAPHY

Books

AXELROD, H. R. and others; *Exotic Tropical Fishes*. T.F.H. Publications, Jersey City, N.J. 1961.

AXELROD, H. R. & L. P. SCHULTZ: *Handbook of Tropical Aquarium Fishes*. McGraw-Hill, New York and London. 1955.

AXELROD, H. R. & WORDERWINKLER: *Encyclopaedia of Tropical Fishes*. T.F.H. Publications, Jersey City, N.J. 1961.

FLETCHER, A. H.: *Unusual Aquarium Fishes*. J. B. Lippincott Co., Philadelphia. 1968.

DUIJN, C. VAN, Jr.: *Diseases of fishes*. Iliffe Books, London. 1967.

HERVEY, G. F. & J. HEMS: *Freshwater tropical fishes*. Batchworth Press, London. 1952.

HERVEY, G. F. & J. HEMS: *The goldfish*. Faber, London. 1968.

INNES, W. T.: *Exotic Aquarium Fishes*. 19th Edition Revised. Aquariums Inc., Maywood, N.J., U.S.A.

JACKMAN, L. A. J.: *Marine aquaria*. David and Charles. Newton Abbot. 1968.

KNOWLES, F. G. W.: *Freshwater and saltwater Aquaria*. Harrap & Co. Ltd., London. 1953.

LAGLER, KARL F., JOHN E. BARDACH, ROBERT R. MILLER: *Ichthyology, the Study of Fishes*. John Wiley and Sons, New York, London. 1962.

MCINERNY, D. & G. GERARD: *All about tropical fish*. Harrap & Co. Ltd., London. 1958.

NORMAN, J. R. & P. H. GREENWOOD: *A history of fishes*. Benn, London. 1963.

STERBA, G.: *Aquarium care*. Studio Vista, London. 1967.

STERBA, G.: *Freshwater fishes of the world*. Studio Vista, London. 1962.

Periodicals

THE AQUARIST AND PONDKEEPER. Buckley Press, London and Brentford, England.

THE AQUARIUM. Pet Books Inc., Maywood, N.J., U.S.A.

TROPICAL FISH HOBBYIST. T.F.H. Publications, Jersey City, N.J., U.S.A. and Reigate, England.

Abudefduf oxyodon 158
– saxatilis 158
Acanthophthalmus kuhlii kuhlii 62
– k. sumatranus 62
– myersi 63
– semicinctus 63
Acanthurus leucosternon 170
Acara, Blue 104
Acorus 187
– calamus v. pusillus 91
– gramineus 126
Aeoliscus strigatus 181
Aequidens curviceps 104
– latifrons 104
– maroni 104
– pulcher 104
Aeration 201
Alestes longipinnis 28
Algae 190
– Blue-green 190
– Green 191
Ambassis lala 100
Amia 148
Amphiprion akallopisos 164
– bicinctus 162
– ephippium 164
– frenatum 164
– laticlavius 164
– percula 162
– perideraion 164
– sebae 162
– xanthurus 162
Ampullaria cuprina 192
Anabantidae 128
Anablepidae 88
Anableps anableps 88
Angelfish 108
– French 156
– Imperial 156
Anoptichthys jordani 22
Anostomidae 44
Anostomus anostomus 44
Anubias 187
– lanceolata 80
– nana 19
Aphanius iberus 70
Aphyocharax rubripinnis 28
Aphyocypris pooni 60
Aphyosemion australe 82

– beauforti 79
– bivittatum 82
– bualanum 82
– calliurum 80
– castaneum 80
– christyi 80
– cinnamomeum 80
– coeruleum 79
– decorsei 80
– elegans 80
– exiguum 82
– fallax 79
– filamentosum 80
– gardneri 80
– gulare 79
– labarrei 82
– multicolor 82
– nigerianum 80
– ruwenzori 80
– schoutedeni 80
– sjoestedti 79
– spurelli 79
– walkeri 79
Apistogramma agassizi 106
– borelli 106
– cactuoides 106
– ortmanni 106
– reitzigi 106
– trifasciatum 106
Aplocheilichthys macrophthalmus 86
Aplocheilus blocki 76
– dayi 76
– lineatus 76
– panchax 76
Apogon maculatus 148
– nematopterus 148
Aponogeton 187
– crispus 187
– ulvaceus 187
– fenestralis 187
Archerfish 140
Argentine Pearl Fish 70
Argus Fish 142
Arnoldichthys spilopterus 38
Arrowhead 189
Artemia salina 209
Astronotus ocellatus 104
Astyanax mexicanus 22
Atherinidae 126
Austrofundulus dolichopterus 86

Bacopa 188
– amplexicaulis 77
– monniera 73
Badis 122

Badis badis 122
Balantiocheilus melanopterus 60
Balistapus undulatus 172
Barb, Black Ruby 48
– Blind 52
– Cherry 51
– China 52
– Five-banded 48
– Golden 52
– Golden Dwarf 50
– Green 52
– Island 50
– Rosy 51
– Schwanenfeld's 52
– Stoliczka's 52
– Sumatra 48
Barbodes 48
Barbus arulius 50
– *conchonius* 51
– *filamentosus* 50
– *gelius* 50
– *nigrofasciatus* 48
– *oligolepis* 50
– *pentazona* 48
– *'schuberti'* 52
– *schwanenfeldi* 52
– *semifasciolatus* 52
– *stoliczkanus* 52
– *tetrazona partipentazona* 48
– *tetrazona tetrazona* 48
– *titteya* 51
Batfish 179
Beacon Fish 30
Bedotia geayi 126
Belonesox belizanus 89
Betta 128
Betta splendens 128
Black Velifera 95
Blennius sphinx 178
Blenny, Sphinx 178
Bloodfin 28
Blue Gularis 79
Blue Puller 158
Bluegill 98
Bluehead 168
Boleophthalmus 143
Botia macracanthus 63
– *modesta* 63
Boxfish, Blue 174
Brachydanio albolineatus 58
– *frankei* 58
– *nigrofasciatus* 58
– *rerio* 58
Brachygobius nunus 124

– *xanthozona* 124
Bumblebee Fish 124
Butterfly Fish 18
Butterflyfish, Long-nosed 152

Cabomba 188
– *caroliniana* 107
– *gigantea* 101
Caecobarbus geertsi 52
Canthigaster valentini 174
Capoeta 48
Caranx speciosus 148
Carassius auratus 54
Cardamine lyrata 136
Cardinal Fish, Pyjama 148
Carinotetraodon somphongsi 138
Carnegiella marthae 46
– *strigata* 46
Catfish, Electric 68
– Glass 64
– Guyana 66
– Paleatus 66
– Upside-down 64
Caudo 90
Caulerpa prolifera 159
Cave-fish, Blind 22
Centrarchidae 98
Centropomidae 100
Centropyge fischeri 158
Ceratopteris 188
– *thalictroides* 56
Chaetodon 98
Chaetodon auriga 155
– *capistratus* 155
– *collaris* 155
– *ephippium* 155
– *melanotus* 154
– *ocellatus* 154
– *octofasciatus* 154
– *vagabundus* 154
Chaetodontoplus mesoleucus 152
Chanda buruensis 100
– *ranga* 100
Characidae 22
Characin, Spraying 26
– Swordtail 26
– Dragon-finned 26
– Long-finned 26
– One-striped African 47
– Red-eyed 38
Cheirodon axelrodi 38
Chelmon rostratus 152
Chilodus punctatus 44
Chlorine 195
Chriopeops goodei 71

Chromide, Orange 120
Chromis caeruleus 158
– *chromis* 158
Cichlasoma biocellatum 104
– *festivum* 102
– *meeki* 102
– *nigrofasciatum* 102
Cichlid, Agassiz's Dwarf 106
– Borelli's Dwarf 106
– Convict 102
– Eye Spot 114
– Firemouth 102
– Golden-eyed Dwarf 104
– Ramirez's Dwarf 106
– Red 112
– Velvet 104
– Yellow Dwarf 106
– Zebra 102
Cichlidae 102
Citharinidae 47
Climbing Perch, Banded 136
Clownfish 162
Cobitidae 62
Colisa chuna 130
– *fasciata* 130
– *labiosa* 131
– *lalia* 130
Copeina, Red-spotted 26
Copeina arnoldi 26
– *guttata* 26
Coralfish, Pennant 150
Corethra 207
Coris angulata 166
– *formosa* 166
– *gaimardi* 166
– *julis* 166
Corydoras, Arched 66
– Black-spotted 66
– Bronze 66
– Dwarf 66
– Leopard 66
– Peppered 66
Corydoras aeneus 66
– *arcuatus* 66
– *hastatus* 66
– *julii* 66
– *melanistius* 66
– *paleatus* 66
Corynopoma riisei 26
Crabs, Horseshoe 184
– King 184
Crassula recurva 75
Cryptocoryne 188
– *aponogetifolia* 115

– *becketti* 121
– *blassi* 133
– *griffithi* 65
– *nevillii* 55
– *petti* 48
– *undulata* 122
– *willisii* 52
Ctenobrycon spilurus 22
Ctenopoma fasciolatum 136
– *oxyrhynchus* 136
Cuttlefish 182
Cyclops 206
Cynolebias belotti 70
– *nigripinnis* 70
– *whitei* 70
Cyprinidae 48
Cyprinodontidae 70

Danio, Giant 58
– Pearl 58
– Spotted 58
– Zebra 58
Danio malabaricus 58
Daphnia 206
Dascyllus aruanus 160
– *carneus* 160
– *marginatus* 160
– *melanurus* 160
– *trimaculatus* 160
Dendrochirus 176
Dermogenys pusillus 98
Diatoms 191
Diodon hystrix 174
Discus 111
– Blue 111
– Brown 111
– Green 111
Dragonfish 176
Dropsy 198

Echidna nebulosa 150
Echinodorus 189
– *berteroi* 37
– *cordifolius* 23
– *longistylis* 30 '
– *paniculatus* 41
– *platense* 39
– *tenellus* 35
Elacatinus oceanops 181
Elassoma evergladei 98
– *okefenokee* 98
– *zonatum* 98
Elodea 189
– *densa* 25
Enchytraeids 207

Epalzeorhynchus kallopterus 60
Epinephelus 146
Epiplatys annulatus 75
– *bifasciatus* 74
– *chaperi* 74
– *dageti monroviae* 74
– *sheljuzhkoi* 74
Eques lanceolatus 148
Etroplus maculatus 120
– *suratensis* 120
Exodon paradoxus 40
Eyes, Bulging 198

Festivum 102
Fighting Fish, Siamese 128
Filtration 201
Fingerfish 144
Fish lice 193
Flagfish, American 70
Flamefish 148
Food 206, 207
– Dried 206
Forceps Fish 152
Forcipiger longirostris 152
Foureyes 88
Fruitflies 207
Fundulus chrysotus 86
Fungus 199

Gambusia affinis 90
Gambusinos 89
Gasteropelecidae 46
Gasteropelecus sternicla 46
Gaterin 90
Girardinus metallicus 90
Gnathonemus petersi 20
– *schilthuisi* 20
Gobiidae 124
Goby, Neon 181
Goldfish 54
Gourami, Chocolate 132
– Croaking 132
– Dwarf 130
– Giant 131
– Kissing 132
– Pearl 134
– Talking 132
– Three-spot 134
Gramma hemichrysos 148
– *loreto* 148
Grammistes sexlineatus 146
Grouper, Golden-striped 146
– Six-lined 146
Guppy 92
Gynochanda filamentosa 100

Gyrinocheilidae 47
Gyrinocheilus aymonieri 47

Halfbeak 98
Haplochromis multicolor 113
Hasemania marginata 28
Hatchetfish, Black-winged 46
– Common 46
– Marbled 46
Hatchetfishes 46
Headstander 44
– Spotted 44
Heating 201
Helisoma nigricans 192
Helostoma temmincki 132
Hemichromis bimaculatus 112
Hemigrammocypris lini 60
Hemigrammus armstrongi 30
– *caudovittatus* 30
– *erythrozonus* 32
– *hyanuary* 30
– *nanus* 32
– *ocellifer* 30
– *pulcher* 30
– *rhodostomus* 32
Hemigymnus melapterus 168
Hemiodontidae 42
Hemirhamphidae 98
Heniochus acuminatus 150
Hermit-crabs 182
Heterandria formosa 90
Heteranthera dubia 94
Hippocampus guttulatus 180
– *hudsonius* 180
– *kuda* 180
– *zosterae* 180
Holacanthus tricolor 156
Hydra 193
Hydrocleis nymphoides 87
Hygrophila polysperma 43
Hyphessobrycon bentosi 34
– *callistus* 34
– *cardinalis* 38
– *copelandi* 34
– *eos* 36
– *flammeus* 32
– *gracilis* 32
– *griemi* 32
– *herbertaxelrodi* 36
– *heterorhabdus* 36
– *innesi* 38
– *metae* 36
– *minor* 34
– *ornatus* 34

– *pulchripinnis* 36
– *roberti* 34
– *rosaceus* 34
– *rubrostigma* 34
– *serpae* 34
– *scholzei* 36

Ichthyophonus 197
Ichthyophthirius multifiliis 195, 196
Infusorians 209
Itch 195

Jack Dempsey 104
Jackknife Fish 148
Java Moss 36
Jewel Fish 112
Jordanella floridae 70
Julidochromis marlieri 120
– *ornatus* 120

Killifish, Ceylon 76
– Golden Ear 86
– Least 90
– Madras 76
Killifishes 70
Killy, Blue-fin 71
Knifefishes 18
Kryptopterus bicirrhis 64

Labeo bicolor 60
Labeotropheus fulleborni 116
– *trewavasae* 116
Labroides dimidiatus 168
Lagarosiphon muscoides 28
Larvae, Midge 207
– Mosquito 207
Leaf-fish, Schomburgk's 122
– South American 122
Lebistes reticulatus 92
Lepomis macrochirus 98
Light, Ultraviolet 212
Lighting 200
Limia, Black-barred 90
– Blue 90
Limia melanogaster 90
– *nigrofasciata* 90
Limnophila heterophylla 130
Limulus polyphemus 185
Lionfish 176
Loach, Clown 63
– Coolie 62
Loricaria filamentosa 68
Loricariidae 68
Ludwigia 189
– *alternifolia* 58

Lutianus sebae 146
Lyretail 82
– Plumed 80
Lythrypnus dalli 181

Macropodus concolor 136
– *cupanus dayi* 136
– *opercularis* 136
Malapteruridae 68
Malapterurus electricus 68
Marcusenius isidori 20
Medaka, Japanese 86
Megalamphodus megalopterus 24
– *sweglesi* 25
Melanotaenia maccullochi 126
– *nigrans* 126
Mesogonistius chaetodon 98
Metals 195
Micralestes interruptus 40
Microgeophagus ramirezi 106
Microspathodon chrysurus 160
Milfoil, Water 92, 189
Minnow, Pike Top 89
– White Cloud Mountain 60
Mochokidae 64
Moenkhausia megalopterus 24
– *oligolepis* 24
– *pittieri* 24
– *sanctae-filomenae* 24
Mollienisia latipinna 94
– *sphenops* 94
– *velifera* 94
Molly, Lyretail 95
Mono 144
Monocirrhus polyacanthus 122
Monodactylidae 144
Monodactylus argenteus 144
– *sebae* 144
Moorish Idol 150
Moray Eel, Starry 150
Mormyridae 20
Mouthbrooder, Egyptian 113
– Mozambique 112
– Small 113
Mullet, Red 152
Mullus surmuletus 152
Muraena helena 150
Myriophyllum 189
– *brasiliense* 128
– *rubrum* 92
– *scabratum* 92
Myripristis murdjan 148

Najas graminea 91
Nandidae 122

Nannacara anomala 104
Nannaethiops tritaeniatus 46
– *unitaeniatus* 47
Nannochromis nudiceps 114
Nannostomus anomalus 42
– *aripirangensis* 42
– *beckfordi* 42
– *eques* 44
– *harrisoni* 42
– *marginatus* 42
– *trifasciatus* 42
Naso brevirostris 170
Neolebias ansorgei 47
Nematobrycon palmeri 40
Neon, Black 36
Neon disease 198
Nitella flexilis 51
Nothobranchius brieni 72
– *guentheri* 72
– *palmquisti* 72
– *rachovii* 72
– *taeniopygus* 72
Notopteridae 18
Notopterus afer 18
Novumbra hubbsi 100
Nymphaea pygmaea 99
– *rubra* 125

Octopus 184
Octopus vulgaris 185
Odonus niger 172
Oodinium 197
Opisthognathus aurifrons 176
Oryzias latipes 86
– *minutillus* 86
Oscar 104
Ostracion lentiginosum 174
Otocinclus flexilis 68
Overcrowding 195
Overfeeding 195
Oxymonacanthus longirostris 172
Ozone 212

Pachypanchax homalonotus 76
– *playfairi* 76
Panchax 76
– Green 76
– Rocket 75
Pantodon buchholzi 18
Pantodontidae 18
Paracanthurus hepatus 170
– *teuthis* 170
Paracheirodon innesi 38
Paradise Fish 136
– Brown Spike-tailed 136

Pelmatochromis kribensis 114
– *pulcher* 114
– *subocellatus* 114
– *thomasi* 114
Pencilfish, Dwarf 42
– Golden 42
– Three-striped 42
– Tube-mouthed 44
Periophthalmidae 142
Periophthalmus koelreuteri 142
Phalloceros caudomaculatus 90
Picasso Fish 172
Pistia stratiotes 143
Planarians 193
Platax orbicularis 178
– *pinnatus* 178
– *teira* 179
Platy 96
– Variatus 96
Plectorhynchus orientalis 150
Plistophora 38
Plotosus anguillaris 176
– *lineatus* 176
Poeciliidae 89
Poisoning 195
Polycentropsis abbeviata 122
Polycentrus schomburgki 122
Pomacanthus annularis 156
– *arcuatus* 156
– *imperator* 156
– *semicirculatus* 156
Pomacentrus melanochir 158
Porcupinefish 174
Premnas biaculeatus 162
Pristella 28
Pristella riddlei 28
Promicrops 146
Pseudocorynopoma doriae 26
Pseudomugil signatus 126
Pseudotropheus auratus 119
– *elongatus* 116
– *fuscus* 119
– *novemfasciatus* 118
– *tropheops* 118
– *zebra* 120
Pterois volitans 176
Pterolebias longipinnis 84
– *peruensis* 84
Pterophyllum altum 108
– *dumerilii* 108
– *eimekei* 108
– *scalare* 108
Pufferfish, Green 138
Puntius 48

222

Pygocentrus 22
Pyrrhulina vittata 28

Quarantine 194

Rainbowfish, Australian Red-tailed 126
– Dwarf 126
Ramirezi 106
Rasbora, Elegant 55
– Eye-spot 56
– Pearly 55
– Red-striped 56
– Scissors-tail 56
Rasbora borapetensis 56
– *dorsiocellata* 56
– *hengeli* 56
– *heteromorpha* 56
– *lateristriata* 55
– *maculata* 56
– *nigromarginata* 55
– *pauciperforata* 56
– *trilineata* 56
– *urophthalma* 56
– *vaterifloris* 55
Razorfish 181
Rhinecanthus aculeatus 172
Riccia fluitans 46
Rivulus, Cuban 84
– Green 84
Rivulus cylindraceus 84
– *harti* 84
– *holmiae* 84
– *milesi* 84
– *urophthalmus* 84
Rock Beauty 156
Roloffia bertholdi 78
– *occidentalis* 78
Rooseveltiella 22

Sagittaria 189
– *chilensis* 82
– *francis* 33
– *subulata f. natans* 84
– *subulata v. pusilla* 139
Sailfish, Celebes 126
Salvinia auriculata 89
Scalare 108
Scat 142
Scatophagidae 142
Scatophagus argus 142
– *rubrifrons* 142
Sea-horse, Golden 180
– Pigmy 180
Sea-perch, Banded 146
Sepia officinalis 185

Serranus scriba 146
Serrasalmus 22
Shark, Red-tailed 60
Shrimp, Brine 209
– Cleaner 182
Shrimpfish 181
Siluridae 64
Siluris glanis 64
Snail, Malayan Mud 193
– Red Ramshorn 192
Snapper, Emperor 146
Spawning 208
Sphaerichthys osphromenoides 132
Stenopus hispidus 182
Striped Anostomus 44
Sunfish, Black-banded 98
– Pigmy 98
Surgeonfish, White-breasted 170
Sweetlip, Oriental 150
Sword Plant, Great Amazon 41
Swordtail 96
Symphysodon aequifasciata aequifasciata 111
– – *axelrodi* 111
– – *haraldi* 111
– *discus* 111
Synnema triflorum 97
Synodontis angelicus 64

Tanichthys albonubes 60
Telmatherina ladigesi 126
Tetra, Black-line 36
– Bleeding Heart 34
– Beunos Aires 30
– Cardinal 38
– Congo 40
– Dawn 36
– Flag 36
– Flame 32
– Glass 24
– Glowlight 32
– Golden 30
– Griem's 32
– Head-and-tail Light 30
– Jewel 34
– Lemon 36
– Loreto 36
– Neon 38
– Pretty 30
– Red-nosed 32
– Rummy-nosed 32
– Silver 22
– Silver-tipped 32

Tetraodon fluviatilis 138
– *palembangensis* 138

Tetraodontidae 138
Tetrosomus gibbosus 174
Thalassoma bifasciatum 168
– *lunare* 168
Thayeria boehlkei 40
– *ifati* 40
– *obliquua* 40
– *sanctae-mariae* 40
Tilapia mossambica 112
– *natalensis* 112
Toothcarps, Egglaying 70
– Livebearing 89
Toxotes jaculator 140
Toxotidae 140
Trichogaster "Cosby" 134
– *leeri* 134
– *microlepis* 134
– *pectoralis* 134
– *trichopterus* 134
Trichopsis pumilus 132
– *vittatus* 132
Tropheus duboisi 120
Tuberculosis, Fish 198
Tubeworms 182
Tubifex 207

Umbra krameri 100
– *limi* 100
– *pygmaea* 100
Umbridae 100

Vallisneria, Corkscrew 21
Vallisneria 189
– *asiatica* 21
– *gigantea* 109
– *spiralis* 67
Vesicularia dubyana 36
Vittata, Striped 28

Water, Choice of 203
– Hardness of 203
– pH of 203, 212
– Salinity of 210, 211
Water Sprite 56
White Cloud 60
White Spot 195
Whiteworms 207
Worm cataract 199
Wrasse, Cleaner 168
– Green 168
– Rainbow 166

Xenomystus nigri 18
Xiphophorus helleri 96

– *maculatus* 96
– *variatus* 96
X-ray Fish 28

Zanclus canescens 150
– *cornutus* 150
Zebra Fish 58
Zebrasoma veliferum 170